# CYBER SECURITY CHALLENGES AND ITS MANAGEMENT STRATEGIES

DR. K. P. MANIKANDAN

# Contents

# Preface

Today, network safety is broadly seen as an issue of squeezing public weightiness. Numerous components of the internet are famously weakly vulnerable to an extending scope of assaults by a range of programmers, evildoers, psychological militants, and verbally express entertainers. For instance, system organizations and private-area organizations both cosmically massive and modest experience the ill effects of digital burglaries of delicate data, digital defacement (e.g., mutilating of Web destinations), and disavowal of-convenience assaults. The country's basic foundation, including the electric power lattice, aviation authority framework, monetary frameworks, and correspondence organizations, relies widely upon data innovation for its activity.

Worries about the defencelessness of the data innovation on which the country depends have extended in the security-cognizant climate after the September 11, 2001, assaults and considering augmented digital surveillance coordinated at privately owned businesses and system organizations in the Cumulated States. Public arrangement creators have become progressively worried that enemies upheld by extensive assets will try to take advantage of the digital susceptibilities in the basic framework, consequently causing significant mischief for the country. Various strategy recommendations have been progressed, and various bills have been acquainted in Congress with tackle parts of the online protection challenge.

# Acknowledgements

Above all, we offer my thanks to our people for giving us an especially lovely environment for doing this undertaking. We wish to convey our certifiable appreciation to the Dr.Vijaya Bhaskar Choudary, Ph.D., Secretary & Correspondent of the Academy for his endeavor in teaching us in this head establishment.

We wish to convey our appreciation and gratefulness to Institutional Head, Dr. C. Yuvaraj and second in order Dr. P. Ramanathan, Vice Principal (Academics), for their help and sincere bearing.

I am elongating my thanks to the Dr.R.Kalpana, HoD of CSE Department for her fortification and showers of benedictions throughout my work to complete my book prosperously.

Our authentic appreciation to all the school staff of Madanapalle Institute of Technology & Science and our allies for their help with the productive perfection of this assignment work.

Finally we bow before God, the almighty who reliably had a prevalent game plan for us. We give our recognition and marvel to Almighty God for successful fulfillment of this endeavor.

CHAPTER ONE

# CyberSecurity - Introduction

**1.1 Network and Security**

Network Security forefends your network and data from breaches, intrusions and other threats. This is a broad and all-encompassing term that refers to hardware and software solutions, as well as processes, rules, and configurations related to network use, accessibility, and overall threat protection.

Access control, virus and antivirus software, application security, network analytics, network-cognate security (endpoint, web, wireless), firewalls, VPN encryption, and other components are all part of network security.

1.1.1.Benefits of Network Security

Network Security is vital in bulwarking client data and information, keeping shared data secure and ascertaining reliable access and network performance as well as aegis from cyber threats. A well designed network security solution abbreviates overhead expenses and safeguards organizations from costly losses that occur from a data breach or other security incident. Ascertaining legitimate access to systems, applications and data enables business operations and distribution of accommodations and products to customers.

1.1.2.Types of Network Security Protections

Firewall

Firewalls control incoming and outgoing traffic on networks, with predetermined security rules. Firewalls keep out inimical traffic and are an obligatory part of daily computing. Network Security relies heavily on Firewalls, and especially Next Generation Firewalls, which fixate on blocking malware and application-layer attacks.

Network Segmentation

Network segmentation defines boundaries between network segments where assets within the group have a mundane function, risk or role within an organization. For instance, the perimeter gateway segments a company network from the Internet. Potential threats outside the network are obviated, ascertaining that an organization's sensitive data remains inside. Organizations can go further by defining supplemental internal boundaries within their network, which can provide amended security and access control.

Access Control

Access control defines the people or groups and the contrivances that have access to network applications and systems thereby gainsaying unsanctioned access, and maybe threats. Integrations with Identity and Access Management (IAM) products can vigorously identify the utilizer and Role-predicated Access Control (RBAC) policies ascertain the person and contrivance are sanctioned access to the asset.

Zero Trust

Remote Access VPN

Remote access VPN provides remote and secure access to a company network to individual hosts or clients, such as telecommuters, mobile users, and extranet consumers. Each host typically has VPN client software loaded or utilizes a web-predicated client. Privacy and integrity of sensitive information is ascertained through multi-factor authentication, endpoint compliance scanning, and encryption of all transmitted data.

Zero Trust Network Access (ZTNA)

The zero trust security model states that a utilizer should only have the access and sanctions that they require to consummate their role. This is a very different approach from that provided by traditional security solutions, like VPNs, that grant a utilizer full access to the target network. Zero trust network access (ZTNA) withal kenned as software-defined perimeter (SDP) solutions sanctions granular access to an organization's applications from users who require that access to perform their obligations.

Email Security

Email security refers to any processes, products, and accommodations designed to bulwark your electronic mail accounts and email content safe from external threats. Most email accommodation providers have built-in email security features designed to keep you secure, but these may not be enough to stop cybercriminals from accessing your information.

Data Loss Prevention (DLP)

Data Loss Prevention (DLP) is a cybersecurity methodology that coalesces technology and best practices to obviate the exposure of sensitive information outside of an organization, especially regulated data such as personally identifiable information (PII) and compliance cognate data: HIPAA, SOX, PCI DSS, etc.

Intrusion Prevention Systems (IPS)

IPS technologies can detect or avert network security attacks such as brute force attacks, Denial of Accommodation (DoS) attacks and exploits of kenned susceptibilities. A susceptibility is an impotency for instance in a software system and an exploit is an assailment that leverages that susceptibility to gain control of that system. When an exploit is promulgated, there is often a window of opportunity for assailers to exploit that susceptibility afore the security patch is applied. An Intrusion Obviation System can be utilized in these cases to expeditiously block these assailments.

Sandboxing

Sandboxing is a cybersecurity practice where you run code or open files in a safe, isolated environment on a host machine that mimics end-utilizer operating environments. Sandboxing optically canvasses the files or code as they are opened and probes for maleficent deportment to avert threats from getting on the network. For example malware in files such as PDF, Microsoft Word, Excel and PowerPoint can be safely detected and blocked afore the files reach an unsuspecting end utilizer.

Hyperscale Network Security

Hyperscale is the faculty of architecture to scale congruously, as incremented demand is integrated to the system. This solution includes expeditious deployment and scaling up or down to meet vicissitudes in network security demands. By tightly integrating networking and compute resources in a software-defined system, it is possible to planarity utilize all hardware resources available in a clustering solution.

Cloud Network Security

Applications and workloads are no longer exclusively hosted on-premises in a local data center. Bulwarking the modern data center requires more preponderant flexibility and innovation to keep pace with the migration of application workloads to the cloud. Software-defined Networking (SDN) and Software-defined Wide Area Network (SD-WAN) solutions enable network security solutions in private, public, hybrid and cloud-hosted Firewall-as-a-Accommodation (FWaaS) deployments.

Robust Network Security

Virus: A virus is a malevolent, downloadable file that can lay dormant that replicates itself by transmuting other computer programs with its own code. Once it spreads those files are infected and can spread from one computer to another, and/or corrupt or eradicate network data.

Worms: Can decelerate computer networks by sharing up bandwidth as well as the slow the efficiency of your computer to process data. A worm is a standalone malware that can propagate and work independently of other files, where a virus needs a host program to spread.

Trojan: A trojan is a backdoor program that engenders an entryway for malignant users to access the computer system by utilizing what looks akin to an authentic program, but expeditiously turns out to be inimical. A trojan virus can expunge files, activate other malware obscue on your computer network, such as a virus and glom valuable data.

Spyware: Much akin to its designation, spyware is a computer virus that accumulates information about a person or organization without their express erudition and may send the information amassed to a third party without the consumer's consent.

Adware: Can redirect your search requests to advertising websites and amass marketing data about you in the process so that customized advertisements will be exhibited predicated on your search and buying history.

Ransomware: This is a type of trojan cyberware that is designed to gain money from the person or organization's computer on which it is installed by encrypting data so that it is unutilizable, blocking access to the user's system.

Secure Your Network With Check Point

Network Security is vital in bulwarking client data and information, it keeps shared data secure, bulwarks from viruses and avails with network performance by truncating overhead expenses and costly losses from data breaches and since there will be less downtime from maleficent users or viruses, it can preserve businesses maxima in the long-term.

Check Point's Network Security solutions simplify your network security without impacting the performance, provide a cumulated approach for streamlined operations, and enable you to scale for business magnification.

Schedule a demo to learn how Check Point forefends customers with efficacious network security for on-premises, branches, and public and private cloud environments.

1.1.3.Network Security Architecture

The architecture of network security models is the result of a well-thought systematic process. While building the architecture, professionals need to keep in mind the type of security the organization requires. Further, they must design several processes, systems, and implements that will avail them avert all sorts of network attacks. The architecture may comprise elements such as access control lists, firewalls, and other types of network security. The network security diagram is given below:

Cyber security Architecture

Every prosperous organization relies on the vigor of its organizational structure. A detailed business plan, efficient employees, and the business experience of key personnel are all critical. A formidable team is built from the consistency and commitment of all of the above, and implementing vigorous cyber security architecture is no exception.

This is how consequential it is to have your organization's cyber security architecture airtight in order to forefend your organization against external threats. Cyber-threats and cyber security breaches come in sundry forms and perpetually evolve. Hence, it is pertinent that an organization like yours is highly security alert and habituated with measures and strategies to militate against possible threats.

Without vigorous security, your organization is vulnerably susceptible to a number of threats. Read on to learn about the purport of cyber security architecture.

Cyber security architecture, additionally kenned as "network security architecture", is a framework that designates the organizational structure, standards, policies and functional demeanor of a computer network, including both security and network features. Cyber security architecture is additionally the manner in which sundry components of your cyber or computer system are organized, synced and integrated.

A cyber security architecture framework is one component of a system's overall architecture. It's designed and built to provide guidance during the design of an entire product/system.

Security architecture avails to position security controls and breach countermeasures and how they relate to the overall systems framework of your company. The main purport of these controls is to maintain your critical system's quality attributes such as confidentiality, integrity and availability. It's withal the synergy between hardware and software erudition with programming proficiency, research skills and policy development.

A security architect is an individual who anticipates potential cyber-threats and is expeditious to design structures and systems to preempt them. Most organizations are exposed to cyber security threats but a cyber security architecture plan avails you to implement and monitor your company's network security systems. A cyber security architecture framework positions all your security controls against any form of malignant actors and how they relate to your overall systems architecture.

Sundry elements of cyber security strategies like firewalls, antivirus programs and intrusion detection systems play an immensely colossal role in bulwarking your organization against external threats. To maintain and maximize these security implements as well as already subsisting and functional policies and procedures, your company should implement a detailed security architecture that integrates these different elements for your networks.

This framework amalgamates sundry methods, processes and implements in order to bulwark an organization's resources, data and other vital information. The prosperity of cyber security architecture relies heavily on the perpetual flow of information throughout the entire organization. Everyone must work according to the framework and processes of your company's security architecture.

1.1.3.1Security Architecture Components

According to Internal Auditors, efficacious and efficient cybersecurity architecture consists of three major components. Those are people, processes and implements that collaborate to bulwark your company's assets. To align these components efficaciously, your security architecture needs to be driven by your security policy. verbalizing your security architecture prospect, implementation plan, and enforcement process.

A security policy is a verbal expression that outlines how each entity accesses each other, what operations sundry entities can carry out, the caliber of bulwark that is required for a system as well as actions that should be taken when these security requisites are not met. The components listed below are a component of efficacious and elaborately orchestrated security architecture:

Direction in the area of incident replication to threats, disaster recuperation, systems configuration, account engenderment and management, and cyber security monitoring.

- Identity management.
- Decided inclusion and omission of those subject to the domain of the security architecture.
- Access and border control.
- Validation and adjustment of the architecture.
- Training.

1.1.3.2.Features of Cyber security Architecture

The following are some of the features of cyber security architecture:

Network Elements

- Network nodes like computers, NICs, repeaters, hubs, bridges, switches, routers, modems, gateways.
- Network communication protocols (TCP/IP, DHCP, DNS, FTP, HTTP, HTTPS, IMAP)
- Network connections between nodes utilizing categorical protocols
- Network topologies among nodes such as point-to-point, circular, chain, and hybrid

Security Elements

- Cybersecurity contrivances like firewalls, Intrusion Detection/Aegis Systems [IDS/IPS], encryption/decryption contrivances.
- Cybersecurity software (anti-virus software, spyware software, anti-malware software)
- Secure network communication protocols (TCP/IP, DHCP, DNS, FTP, HTTP, HTTPS, IMAP).

- Vigorous encryption techniques like end-to-end encryption, zero-erudition privacy, blockchain.

Security Frameworks & Standards

- Cybersecurity framework architecture standards like NIST Risk Management Framework (RMF) SP 800-37 and ISO IEC 27000-Series.
- Technology standards for cybersecurity software culls.

Security Procedures & Policies

These are security procedures and policies directed towards your organization and enforced. According to Cybersecurity Forum, a cybersecurity architecture should ideally be definable and simulatable utilizing an industry-standard architecture modeling language (e.g., SysML, UML2).

Key Phases in Security Architecture

These are the key phases in the security architecture framework and process:

Architecture Risk Assessment: Here, you evaluate the influence of vital business assets, the jeopardies, and the effects of susceptibilities and security threats to your organization.

Security Architecture and Design: At this phase, the design and architecture of security accommodations are structured to avail the aegis of your organization's assets in order to facilitate business risk exposure objectives and goals.

Implementation: Cyber security accommodations and processes are operated, implemented, monitored and controlled. The architecture is designed to ascertain that the security policy and standards, security architecture decisions, and imperil management are plenarily implemented and efficacious for a long period.

Operations and Monitoring: Here, measures like threat and susceptibility management and threat management are taken to monitor, supervise and handle the operational state in integration to examining the impact of the system's security.

Purport of Cyber security Architecture

The purport of cybersecurity architecture is simply to ascertain that the main network architecture of your company including sensitive data and critical applications are planarity for fended against any present or future threats and breaches. It's consequential you planarity understand the sundry impotent points in your system in order to efficaciously and expeditiously proffer a solution.

The best way to identify your system's impuissant point is to employ the accommodations of a cybersecurity architect. A cybersecurity architect will exhaustively evaluate surface susceptibilities for different network topologies and cyber-attacks to efficaciously bulwark your sensitive data and critical applications.

The primary goals of efficacious cybersecurity architecture are:

To ascertain that all cyber-assailments are minimized, mitigated against, obscure or dynamic.

To ascertain that cyber-attack surfaces should be relatively minuscule in size, covertly stored, so that they are stealth in moving towards threat targets and arduous for cyber threats to detect and perforate.

To ascertain that confidential and sensitive data is vigorously encrypted, and be subject to culminate-to-end encryption techniques during transfer.

All cyber-assailments are aggressively detected, mitigated, and contravened utilizing countermeasures like Moving-Target Defences (MTD).

Cybersecurity architects are concretely adroit in identifying potential threats. They understand computer and network systems enough to design security architecture plans, implement these orchestrations, and supervise the opportune implementation.

**1.2 Information Assurance Model in Cyber Security**

Information Assurance concerns implementation of methods that fixated on forfending and safeguarding critical information and germane information systems by assuring confidentiality, integrity, availability, and non-repudiation. It is strategic approach focused which focuses more on deployment of policies rather than building infrastructures.

1. Information Assurance Model

The security model is multidimensional model predicated on four dimensions :

1. Information States

Information is referred to as interpretation of data which can be found in three states stored, processed, or transmitted.

3. Security Accommodations

It is fundamental pillar of the model which provides security to system and consists of five accommodations namely availability, integrity, confidentiality, authentication, and non-repudiation.

4. Security Countermeasures

This dimension has functionalities to preserve system from immediate susceptibility by accounting for technology, policy & practice, and people.

5. Time

This dimension can be viewed in many ways. At any given time data may be available offline or online, information and system might be in flux thus, introducing risk of unauthorized access. Ergo, in every phase of System Development Cycle, every aspect of Information Assurance model must be well defined and well implemented in order to minimize risk of unauthorized access.

### 1.2.1.Information States

1. Transmission

It defines time wherein data is between processing steps.

Example :

In transit over networks when utilizer sends email to reader, including recollection and storage encountered during distribution.

2. Storage

It defines time during which data is preserved on medium such as hard drive.Example: Preserving document on file server's disk by utilizer.

3. Processing

It defines time during which data is in processing state.

Example :

Data is processed in desultory access recollection (RAM) of workstation.

1.2.2.Security Accommodations

1. Confidentiality

It assures that information of system is not disclosed to unauthorized access and is read and interpreted only by persons sanctioned to do so. Bulwark of confidentiality obviates maleficent access and contingent disclosure of information. Information that is considered to be confidential is called as sensitive information.

To ascertain confidentiality data is categorized into different categories according to damage astringency and then accordingly rigorous measures are taken.

Example :

Forefending email content to read by only desired set of users. This can be insured by data encryption. Two-factor authentication, vigorous passwords, security tokens, and biometric verification are some popular norms for authentication users to access sensitive data.

2. Integrity

It ascertains that sensitive data is precise and trustworthy and can not be engendered, transmuted, or effaced without opportune sanction. Maintaining integrity involves modification or ravagement of information by unauthorized access.

To ascertain integrity backups should be orchestrated and implemented in order to instaurate any affected data in case of security breach. Besides this cryptographic checksum can withal be utilized for verification of data.

Example :

Implementation of measures to verify that e-mail content was not modified in transit. This can be achieved by utilizing cryptography which will ascertain that intended utilizer receives correct and precise information.

3. Availability

It assures reliable and constant access to sensitive data only by sanctioned users. It involves measures to sustain access to data in spite of system failures and sources of interference.

To ascertain availability of corrupted data must be eliminated, recuperation time must be expedite and physical infrastructure must be ameliorated.

Example :

Accessing and throughput of e-mail accommodation.

4. Authentication

It is security accommodation that is designed to establish validity of transmission of message by verification of individual's identity to receive categorical category of information.

To ascertain availability of sundry single factors and multi-factor authentication methods are utilized. A single factor authentication method uses single parameter to verify users' identity whereas two-factor authentication uses multiple factors to verify user's identity.

Example :

Entering username and password when we authenticate in to website is example of authentication. Entering correct authentication lets website verify our identity and ascertains that only we access sensitive information.

5. Non-Repudiation

It is mechanism to ascertain sender or receiver cannot gainsay fact that they are a component of data transmission. When sender sends data to receiver, it receives distribution substantiation. When receiver receives message it has all information affixed within message regarding sender.

Example :

A prevalent example is sending SMS from one mobile phone to another. After message is received corroboration message is exhibited that receiver has received message. In reciprocation, message received by receiver contains all information about sender.

Security Countermeasures :

1. People

People are heart of information system. Administrators and users of information systems must follow policies and practice for designing good system. They must be apprised conventionally regarding information system and yare to act felicitously to safeguard system.

2. Policy & Practice

Every organization has some set of rules defined in form of policies that must be followed by every individual working in organization. These policies must be practiced in order to opportunely handle sensitive information whenever system gets compromised.

3. Technology

Felicitous technology such as firewalls, routers, and intrusion detection must be utilized in order to forfend system from susceptibilities, threats. The technology used must facilitate expeditious replication whenever information security gets compromised.

**1.3 Cyber Security Threats and Strategy**

## *1.3.1.Threat in Cybersecurity*

A cybersecurity threat is a maleficent and deliberate attack by an individual or organization to gain unauthorized access to another individual's or organization's network to damage, disrupt, or purloin IT assets, computer networks, perspicacious property, or any other form of sensitive data.

1.3.1.1.Types of Cybersecurity Threats

While the types of cyber threats perpetuate to grow, there are some of the most mundane and prevalent cyberthreats that present-day organizations need to ken about. The top 10 cyber security threats are as follows:

1) Malware

Malware assailments are the most prevalent cyber security threats. Malware is defined as malignant software, including spyware, ransomware, viruses, and worms, which gets installed into the system when the utilizer clicks a hazardous link or email. Once inside the system, malware can block access to critical components of the network, damage the system, and amass confidential information, among others.

2) Phishing

Cybercriminals send malignant electronically mails that seem to emanate from legitimate resources. The utilizer is then illuded into clicking the malignant link in the electronic mail, leading to malware installation or disclosure of sensitive information like credit card details and authenticate credentials.

3) Spear Phishing

Spear phishing is a more sophisticated form of a phishing attack in which cybercriminals target only privileged users such as system administrators and C-suite executives.

4) Man in the Middle Attack

Man in the Middle (MitM) attack occurs when cyber malefactors place themselves between a two-party communication. Once the assailant interprets the communication, they may filter and purloin sensitive data and return different replications to the utilizer.

5) Denial of Accommodation Attack

Denial of Accommodation attacks aims at flooding systems, networks, or servers with massive traffic, thereby making the system unable to consummate legitimate requests. Attacks can withal utilize several infected contrivances to launch an assailment on the target system. This is kenned as a Distributed Denial of Accommodation (DDoS) attack.

6) SQL Injection

A Structured Query Language (SQL) injection attack occurs when cybercriminals endeavor to access the database by uploading malignant SQL scripts. Once prosperous, the malevolent actor can view, change, or expunge data stored in the SQL database.

7) Zero-day Exploit

A zero-day attack occurs when software or hardware susceptibility is promulgated, and the cybercriminals exploit the susceptibility afore a patch or solution is implemented.

8) Advanced Sedulous Threats (APT)

An advanced assiduous threat occurs when a malignant actor gains unauthorized access to a system or network and remains undetected for an elongated time.

9) Ransomware

Ransomware is a type of malware attack in which the assailer locks or encrypts the victim's data and threatens to publish or block access to data unless a ransom is paid. Learning more about ransomware threats can avail companies obviate and cope with them preponderant.

10) DNS Attack

A DNS assailment is a cyberattack in which cybercriminals exploit susceptibilities in the Domain Name System (DNS). The assailers leverage the DNS susceptibilities to divert site visitors to maleficent pages (DNS Hijacking) and abstract data from compromised systems (DNS Tunneling).

Cyber Threat Actors

In order to respond efficaciously to a cyberattack, it's imperative to ken the threat actors and understand their tactics, techniques, and procedures.

Here are some of the mundane sources of cyber threats:

1) Nation States

Cyber attacks by a nation can inflict detrimental impact by disrupting communications, military activities, and everyday life.

2)Criminal Groups

Malefactor groups aim to infiltrate systems or networks for financial gain. These groups use phishing, spam, spyware, and malware to conduct identity larceny, online fraud, and system extortion.

3) Hackers

Hackers explore sundry cyber techniques to breach bulwarks and exploit susceptibilities in a computer system or network. They are incentivized by personal gain, revenge, stalking, financial gain, and political activism. Hackers develop incipient types of threats for the thrill of challenge or gasconading rights in the hacker community.

4) Terrorist Groups

Terrorists conduct cyber attacks to eradicate, infiltrate, or exploit critical infrastructure to threaten national security, compromise armaments, disrupt the economy, and cause mass casualties.

5) Hacktivists

Hacktivists carry out cyberattacks in support of political causes rather than for financial gain. They target industries, organizations, or individuals who don't align with their political conceptions and agenda.

6) Malicious Intruders

97% of surveyed IT bellwethers expressed concerns about insider threats in cyber security. Insiders can include employees, third-party vendors, contractors, or other business associates who have legitimate access to enterprise assets but misuse that accesses to purloin or ravage information for financial or personal gain.

7) Corporate Spies

Corporate spies conduct industrial or business espionage to either make a profit or disrupt a competitor's business by assailing critical infrastructure, purloining trade secrets, and gaining access.

### *1.3.2.Cyber Security Strategies*

To design and implement a secure cyberspace, some stringent strategies have been put in place that are given below

- Creating a Secure Cyber Ecosystem
- Creating an Assurance Framework

- Encouraging Open Standards
- Strengthening the Regulatory Framework
- Creating Mechanisms for IT Security
- Securing E-governance Services
- Protecting Critical Information Infrastructure

Strategy 1 – Engendering a Secure Cyber Ecosystem

The cyber ecosystem involves a wide range of varied entities like contrivances (communication technologies and computers), individuals, regimes, private organizations, etc., which interact with each other for numerous reasons.

This strategy explores the conception of having a vigorous and robust cyber-ecosystem where the cyber-contrivances can collaborate with each other in the future to obviate cyber-attacks, minimize their efficacy, or find solutions to recuperate from a cyber-attack.

Such a cyber-ecosystem would have the competency built into its cyber contrivances to sanction secured ways of action to be organized within and among groups of contrivances. This cyber-ecosystem can be supervised by present monitoring techniques where software products are acclimated to detect and report security impuissances.

A vigorous cyber-ecosystem has three symbiotic structures – Automation, Interoperability, and Authentication.

Automation – It facilitates the implementation of advanced security measures, enhances the swiftness, and optimizes the decision-making processes.

Interoperability – It toughens the collaborative actions, ameliorates vigilance, and expedites the cognition procedure. There are three types of interoperability –

Semantic (i.e., shared lexicon predicated on prevalent understanding)

Technical

Policy – Consequential in assimilating different contributors into an inclusive cyber-bulwark structure.

Authentication – It amends the identification and verification technologies that work in order to provide –

- Security
- Affordability
- Ease of avail and administration

- Scalability
- Interoperability

Strategy 2 – Creating an Assurance Framework

The objective of this strategy is to design an outline in compliance with the ecumenical security standards through traditional products, processes, people, and technology.

To cater to the national security requisites, a national framework kenned as the Cybersecurity Assurance Framework was developed. It accommodates critical infrastructure organizations and the regimes through "Enabling and Endorsing" actions.

Enabling actions are performed by regime entities that are autonomous bodies liberate from commercial intrigues. The publication of "National Security Policy Compliance Requisites" and IT security guidelines and documents to enable IT security implementation and compliance are done by these ascendant entities.

Endorsing actions are involved in remuneratively lucrative accommodations after meeting the obligatory qualification standards and they include the following –

ISO 27001/BS 7799 ISMS certification, IS system audits etc., which are essentially the compliance certification.

'Prevalent Criteria' standard ISO 15408 and Crypto module verification standards, which are the IT Security product evaluation and certification.

Accommodations to avail consumers in implementation of IT security such as IT security manpower training.

Trusted Company Certification

Indian IT/ITES/BPOs need to comply with the international standards and best practices on security and privacy with the development of the outsourcing market. ISO 9000, CMM, Six Sigma, Total Quality Management, ISO 27001 etc., are some of the certifications.

Subsisting models such as SEI CMM levels are exclusively betokened for software development processes and do not address security issues. Ergo, several efforts are made to engender a model predicated on self-certification concept and on the lines of Software Capability Maturity Model (SW-CMM) of CMU, USA.

The structure that has been engendered through such sodality between industry and regime, comprises of the following –

standards

guidelines

practices

These parameters avail the owners and operators of critical infrastructure to manage cybersecurity-cognate peril.

Strategy 3 – Encouraging Open Standards

Standards play a paramount role in defining how we approach information security cognate issues across geographical regions and societies. Open standards are inspirited to –

Enhance the efficiency of key processes,

Enable systems incorporations,

Provide a medium for users to quantify incipient products or accommodations,

Organize the approach to arrange incipient technologies or business models,

Interpret intricate environments, and

Endorse economic magnification.

Standards such as ISO 27001[3] enhearten the implementation of a standard organization structure, where customers can understand processes, and abbreviate the costs of auditing.

Strategy 4 – Strengthening the Regulatory Framework

The objective of this strategy is to engender a secure cyberspace ecosystem and fortify the regulatory framework. A 24X7 mechanism has been envisioned to deal with cyber threats through National Critical Information Infrastructure Bulwark Centre (NCIIPC). The Computer Emergency Replication Team (CERT-In) has been designated to act as a nodal agency for crisis management.

Some highlights of this strategy are as follows –

Promotion of research and development in cybersecurity.

Developing human resource through edification and training programs.

Inspiriting all organizations, whether public or private, to designate a person to accommodate as Chief Information Security Officer (CISO) who will be responsible for cybersecurity initiatives.

Indian Armed Forces are in the process of establishing a cyber-command as a component of fortifying the cybersecurity of bulwark network and installations.

Efficacious implementation of public-private partnership is in pipeline that will go a long way in engendering solutions to the ever-transmuting threat landscape.

Strategy 5 – Creating Mechanisms for IT Security

Some fundamental mechanisms that are in place for ascertaining IT security are – link-oriented security measures, end-to-end security measures, sodality-oriented measures, and data encryption. These methods differ in their internal application features and withal in the attributes of the security they provide. Let us discuss them in brief.

Link-Oriented Measures

It distributes security while transferring data between two nodes, irrespective of the eventual source and destination of the data.

End-to-End Measures

It is a medium for conveying Protocol Data Units (PDUs) in a bulwarked manner from source to destination in such a way that disruption of any of their communication links does not breach security.

Sodality-Oriented Measures

Sodality-oriented measures are a modified set of end-to-end measures that forfend every sodality individually.

Data Encryption

It defines some general features of conventional ciphers and the recently developed class of public-key ciphers. It encodes information in a way that only the sanctioned personnel can decrypt them.

Strategy 6 – Securing E-governance Services

Electronic governance (e-governance) is the most treasured instrument with the regime to provide public accommodations in an accountable manner. Lamentably, in the current scenario, there is no devoted licit structure for e-governance in India.

Similarly, there is no law for obligatory e-distribution of public accommodations in India. And nothing is more hazardous and onerous than executing e-governance projects without adequate cybersecurity. Hence, securing the e-governance accommodations has become a crucial task, especially when the nation is making daily transactions through cards.

Fortuitously, the Reserve Bank of India has implemented security and imperil mitigation measures for card transactions in India enforceable from 1st October, 2013. It has put the responsibility of ascertaining secured card transactions upon banks rather than on customers.

"E-regime" or electronic regime refers to the utilization of Information and Communication Technologies (ICTs) by regime bodies for the following –

Efficient distribution of public accommodations

Refining internal efficiency

Facile information exchange among denizens, organizations, and regime bodies

Re-structuring of administrative processes.

Strategy 7 – Protecting Critical Information Infrastructure

Critical information infrastructure is the backbone of a country's national and economic security. It includes power plants, highways, bridges, chemical plants, networks, as well as the buildings where millions of people work every day. These can be secured with stringent collaboration plans and disciplined implementations.

Safeguarding critical infrastructure against developing cyber-threats needs a structured approach. It is required that the regime aggressively collaborates with public and private sectors on a customary substructure to obviate, respond to, and coordinate mitigation efforts against endeavored disruptions and adverse impacts to the nation's critical infrastructure.

It is in demand that the regime works with business owners and operators to reinforce their accommodations and groups by sharing cyber and other threat information.

A prevalent platform should be shared with the users to submit comments and conceptions, which can be collaborated to build a tougher substratum for securing and bulwarking critical infrastructures.

The regime of USA has passed an executive order "Ameliorating Critical Infrastructure Cybersecurity" in 2013 that prioritizes the management of cybersecurity peril involved in the distribution of critical infrastructure accommodations. This Framework provides a mundane relegation and mechanism for organizations to –

Define their subsisting cybersecurity bearing,

Define their objectives for cybersecurity,

Categorize and prioritize chances for development within the framework of a constant process, and

Communicate with all the investors about cybersecurity.

CHAPTER TWO

# Blockchain security vulnerabilities

## 2.1. Introduction

Blockchain is a data structure, or Distributed Ledger Technology (DLT), that records transactions between multiple computers, ascertaining more security, transparency, and decentralization for utilizer and company operations. The blocks of data are interconnected, composing a chain of records controlled by no single ascendancy and open to any and every member of the blockchain.

Thus, the chances of fraudulent activity or duplication of transactions are eliminated without the desideratum of a third party.

Once information is stored on the blockchain, it's immutable. The blockchain secures each transaction with a digital signature that proves its authenticity. Through the technology's encryption and digital signatures, the data stored is tamper-proof and cannot be transmuted.

Any industry can utilize blockchain. This is because any digital asset or transaction can be inserted into the blockchain. The incipient technology is considered a reliable cybersecurity protocol due to its capabilities of designating any foul play and providing certainty in the integrity of transactions

Blockchain is predicated on the conceptions of consensus, decentralization, and cryptography to ascertain transaction trust. However, many blockchain security issues have arisen due to faulty technology implementation.

Without a doubt, blockchain technology has grown in popularity in recent years. Apart from its initial application in cryptocurrency, it is now being utilized in healthcare, authentic estate, astute contacts, and other fields.

Blockchain technology accumulates and stores data in groupings kenned as “blocks,” and each block can hold a set quantity of data. When a block is plenary, it is chained to the anterior full block, composing a data chain, hence the brilliant name “blockchain.”

The technology has been a great example of how security tenets in financial transactions and information transmission are transformed. It provides a one-of-a-kind data structure as well as built-in security features. Blockchain is predicated on the conceptions of consensus, decentralization, and cryptography to ascertain transaction trust.

However, many blockchain security issues have arisen due to faulty technology implementation.

### 2.2. Benefits of Blockchain Security

The advantages of blockchain revolve around one of its main characteristics – decentralization, ascertaining a higher caliber of data integrity throughout multiple operations.

2.2.1.Decentralization of Storage Systems

In recent years, there have been millions of cyber attacks on organizations. And one mundane element between all the organizations is that they utilized a centralized system. This denotes that a hacker can access a substantial magnitude of a company’s critical data in one place (Source: Medium).

2.2.2. Utilizing Blockchain Security to Decentralize Storage Systems

Take, for example, the WannaCry ransomware attack in 2017. The assailments impacted roughly 230,000 computers in 150 countries. WannaCry targeted vulnerably susceptible computers that had yet to update their Microsoft Windows operating system (Source: Kaspersky).

Once inside the computers, assailers glommed utilizer information, which would be returned for a ransom. Albeit there's no assurance, if not paid, hackers would sempiternally efface the data. It's estimated that the WannaCry ransomware attack caused $4 billion in losses across the globe.

Shifting to decentralized systems is a way to obviate ransomware, like WannaCry, from capitalizing on a single susceptibility point in a computer.

With a centralized system, data is typically stored, updated, and managed through one location rather than spread out across many. In contrast, with a decentralized system, data germane to respective sites are stored and maintained independently of a central hub. (Source: Medium)

Blockchain complies with this rule with data spread across multiple computers. Since the same data is distributed and synchronized in several independent locations, the prospect of hacking the entire system makes cyber assailing intricate and cumbersome.

2.2.3.IoT Security

Edge contrivances such as mobile phones, cameras, routers, and switches are becoming a point of interest for hackers. With technologies like artificial perspicacity (AI) and 5G enabling the magnification of the Internet of Things (IoT), if a malevolent threat gains access to one contrivance, it can compromise your entire system.

2.2.3.1.Blockchain Security Benefits IoT Security

Understand how 5G's impact on IoT-enabled applications is leading us into the future. Read our blog, The Perspicacious Cities of Tomorrow Enabled by 5G and IoT.

Organizations can utilize blockchain to secure interconnected contrivances and systems by decentralizing their administration. Blockchain technology gives contrivances the capability to make security decisions on their own by analyzing the network and composing a consensus on what constitutes customary and suspicious activity in the chain (Source: Forbes). In essence, each point in the blockchain is another hurdle for the hacker to apostatize in lieu of having one central administration or ascendancy for the cyber attack to surmount.

IoT Applications have incremented the authoritative ordinance for more vigorous security solutions. CENGN works with Canadian SMEs to test and validate innovative network security approaches to ascertain modern and future networks remain forfended from cyberattacks. Ascertain how we can avail on our Security page.

**2.3.Secure Messaging Communication**

The advancement of our networks has led to an evolution of how we communicate. Currently, organizations send messages through multiple digital channels sanctioning the transfer of sundry file formats. This flexibility has amended engenderment and collaboration but has additionally brought its risks through incremented susceptibility points.

2.3.1.Securing message communications

To maintain secure networks, message platform developers implement end-to-end encryption (E2EE) in their applications. This method encrypts information so that only the players engaged in communication can read the messages, omitting Internet accommodation providers, the app developer, the regime, or anyone else (Source: Stream).

Blockchain can build on the advantages of current E2EE solutions, developing an even more secure environment for users. Blockchain can enable cross-herald communication capabilities through a standard security protocol, sanctioning for a cumulated API framework that secures all data exchange processes (Source: Cyber Management Coalition).

For example, Sense Chat is a blockchain-enabled messaging platform that operates over subsisting accommodations like Kik, WeChat, Slack, Skype, Facebook Herald, and beyond (Source: Disruptor Daily). Features include innominate connections, peer-to-peer video, and crypto-convivial messaging.

**2.4. Blockchain Security According To Blockchain Type**

To further expound blockchain security, it is compulsory to first grasp the distinction between public and private blockchain security. In terms of participation and data access capabilities, blockchain networks can have sundry effects. As a result, there are two forms of labeling for blockchain networks.

Blockchain networks can be private or public, depending on the privileges required for membership. The expedient for participants to acquire access to the network, on the other hand, are governed by whether the blockchain network is permissioned or permissionless.

• Public blockchain networks are open and might sanction any utilizer to join while maintaining participant anonymity.

• In private blockchain networks, identity is utilized to substantiate membership and access privileges. Furthermore, they only sanction familiar organizations to participate.

2.4.1.Five Blockchain Security Issues And Solutions

Many people are right when they believe blockchain is inherently secure. Blockchain is incontrovertibly salutary to organizations, but it has paramount drawbacks due to categorical security issues. Here are five of the top blockchain security challenges and their solutions.

1. 51% ATTACKS

Miners play a consequential role in validating transactions on the blockchain, sanctioning them to develop even further. A 51% assailment is possibly the most dreaded threat in the entire blockchain business. These assailments are more liable to occur in the chain's early stage, and a 51% attack does not apply to enterprise or private blockchains.

A 51% attack occurs when a single individual or organization (malevolent hackers) accumulates more than a moiety of the hash rate and seizes control of the entire system, which can be disastrous. Hackers can modify the order of transactions and avert them from being substantiated. They can even invert antecedently consummated transactions, resulting in double-spending.

To obviate 51% attacks:

• Ameliorate mining pool monitoring.

• Make certain that the hash rate is higher.

• Evade utilizing proof-of-work (PoW) consensus procedures.

2. PHISHING ATTACKS

Phishing attacks on blockchain networks are incrementing, causing earnest issues. Individuals or company employees are frequently the targets of phishing endeavors.

The hacker's goal in a phishing assailment is to purloin the user's credentials. They can send legitimate-looking emails to the owner of the wallet key. The utilizer is required to enter authenticate details via an annexed fake hyperlink. Having access to a user's credentials and other sensitive information might result in damages for both the utilizer and the blockchain network. They are additionally vulnerably susceptible to follow-up attacks.

To obviate phishing attacks:

• Amend browser security by installing a verified integrate-on to notify you about unsafe websites.

• Amend contrivance security by installing malignant link detection software as well as dependable antivirus software.

• Reconfirm with the partner if you receive an electronic mail requesting authenticate details relating to the issue.

• Don't click on the link until you have exhaustively reviewed it. In lieu of clicking on the links, enter the address into your browser.

• Eschew open Wi-Fi networks when utilizing an electronic wallet or other paramount banking transactions.

• Ascertain your system and software are au courant.

3. ROUTING ATTACKS

The next major concern for blockchain technology's security and privacy is routing attacks.

A blockchain network and application rely on the authentic-time kineticism of massive magnitudes of data. Hackers can utilize an account's anonymity to intercept data as it is being transmitted to internet accommodation providers.

In the case of a routing attack, blockchain participants are customarily incognizant of the threat because data transmission and operations proceed as customary. The jeopardy is that these assailments will frequently expose confidential data or extract currency without the user's erudition.

To obviate routing attacks:

• Implementat secure routing protocols (with certificates).

• Use data encryption.

• Change passwords conventionally; use vigorous passwords.

• Edify yourself and your employees about the hazards associated with information security.

4. BLOCKCHAIN ENDPOINT SUSCEPTIBILITIES

The susceptibility of blockchain endpoints is another paramount security concern in blockchain security.

The blockchain network's endpoint is where users interact with the blockchain: on electronic contrivances such as computers and mobile phones. Hackers can optically canvass utilizer comportment and target contrivances to glom the user's key. This is one of the most visible blockchain security issues.

To obviate endpoint susceptibilities:

• Do not preserve blockchain keys on your computer or mobile phone as text files.

• Download and install antivirus software for your electronic contrivances.

• Review the system customarily, keeping track of the time, location, and contrivance access.

5. SYBIL ATTACKS

In a Sybil attack, hackers engender numerous fake network nodes. Utilizing those nodes, the hacker can obtain majority consensus and disrupt the chain's transactions. As a result, an immensely colossal-scale Sybil assault is nothing more than a 51% attack.

To obviate Sybil attacks:

• Use felicitous consensus algorithms.

• Monitor other nodes' demeanor and check for the nodes that are only forwarding blocks from one utilizer.

While these algorithms may not exhaustively obviate these assailments, they make them infeasible for the hacker to carry out.

**2.5. Value Traits in Blockchain Technology**

Blockchain technology is open, shared, and highly secure. Any transaction on the network is visible to all participants. However, the sanctioned participants could only access a transaction on the blockchain. So, it is ineluctably foreordained to wonder about the secret ingredient that can keep blockchain technology going in the future? Any blockchain presage for the future would conspicuously depend on the value advantage it distributes to enterprises. Let us take a visual examination of the unique elements which define the value of blockchain technology.

1. Trust

Users could integrate incipient information to the blockchain ledger only after the approbation of a majority of network participants. Network participants provide approbation for transactions after they get reliable proof of that the fact that the cryptographically transmitted information is veritable.

2. Immutability and Transparency

The next consequential traits which would determine the future of blockchain include immutability and transparency. Immutability suggests that incipient information could be integrated on a blockchain only to the precedent data. In integration, it is infeasible to modify or lose information once it is integrated to the blockchain network. Transparency is conspicuous in blockchain with the fact that any network participant could audit the transmutations on the ledger.

3. Paramount Ameliorations

The value benefits of blockchain technology in cost savings and ameliorating the haste of transactions are pellucidly ascendant highlights. Blockchain could avail in taking away intermediaries, thereby offering promising cost abbreviation benefits. In additament, blockchain can enable business transactions at any time without any setbacks. Most consequential of all, blockchain facilitates better speed in transactions involving mazuma or other assets.

4. Decentralization

The most critical factor for the future of blockchain technology would conspicuously point towards decentralization. The blockchain ledger is not under the maintenance of a particular individual, governance, or company. On the contrary, all the computers participating in the network take care of the maintenance of the blockchain network. Ergo, any two parties could engage in transactions without any centralized ascendancy for establishing trust for the transaction.

**2.6.Subsisting Applications of Blockchain**

The potential of blockchain is genuinely massive. However, there are many doubts regarding how blockchain would fare in the future. So, it is paramount to draw an impression of the sundry industries which have been through a positive transformation with blockchain. One of the eminent examples of enterprise blockchain platforms that have gained radical popularity is IBM blockchain. The different subsisting applications could give a glimpse of the blockchain future prospects. Here are some of the eminent use cases of IBM blockchain.

INBLOCK utilizes IBM LinuxONE for addressing cryptocurrency technical issues. As a result, it can ascertain better accomodation, safety, and speed with digital asset transactions.

Plastic Bank leverages a blockchain banking platform running on the IBM cloud for offering a high-security, scalable reward system for amassing and recycling plastic.

The leading grocery retailer in the US, Kroger, utilizes IBM Victuals Trust for working with suppliers on tracing aliment from farm to store shelves.

Spotify utilizes blockchain for managing copyrights.

Eastman Kodak depends on blockchain-predicated accommodations for engendering storage for stock photos.

Consequently, it is limpidly conspicuous that all the blockchain presages till now have come veridical. It has transformed the way we perceive financial transactions and the security of information exchange across public networks. Furthermore, blockchain additionally presents cost benefits and value for enterprises with better scope for scalability. However, it is additionally plausible to fixate on the future trends expected with blockchain technology. The future trends can provide a clear impression of the way people and businesses would perceive blockchain in the future

**2.7.Future of Blockchain Technology – Latest Trends**

The world witnessed a radical shift in virtually every field, starting from governance to manufacturing after an ecumenical pandemic. People were restricted to the confines of their homes, and ecumenical corporate organizations had to run their operations remotely. Concurrently, the drive for digital transformation additionally gained momentum, thereby calling for the adoption of blockchain technology. However, it is plausible to fixate on the feasibility of blockchain in the long run. Let us take an optical canvassing of some of the top trends about the future of blockchain.

2.7.1. Demand for Blockchain Expertise Perpetuates to Escalate

As the world apperceives the potential of blockchain technology, enterprises would require professionals with the right blockchain skills and cognizance. However, the popularity of blockchain as a technology has not affected the supply of blockchain aptitude. The online freelancing platform, Upwork, has recently reported a radical magnification in demand for people with blockchain expertise. Since the technology is comparatively incipient with circumscribed vigilance, it is arduous to find a plethora of blockchain engineers.

Consequently, the blockchain future definitely holds some lucrative vocation opportunities for aspiring professionals. The massive adeptness gap for blockchain technology withal ascertains the scope for better remuneration of blockchain professionals. With the right professional training and certification for particular blockchain job roles, you can score a promising blockchain vocation in the future.

2.7.2.Incipient Governance Models

The blockchain landscape is growing radically, and incipient governance models are the desideratum of the hour. So, how will these incipient governance models work? You can visually examine governance models capable of enabling massive and diverse consortia for better efficiency in decision-making, payments, and permissioning schemes. The incipient governance models will rightly be the future of blockchain technology by ascertaining the standardization of information from sundry sources.

In additament, the incipient governance models can avail in amassing incipient and more resilient data sets. Virtually 68% of CIOs and CTOs perceive the desideratum for a scalable governance model to fortify interactions over multiple blockchain networks. The scalable governance model is an obligatory feature that will be optically discerned in the blockchain environment of organizations in the coming years.

2.7.3.The Blockchain-IoT Connection

Coalescing other technologies with blockchain can avail us in achieving many promising milestones. Blockchain can offer credible data for apprising and reinforcing underlying algorithms of adjacent technologies. In additament, blockchain could additionally ascertain data security alongside a comprehensively detailed audit of each step in the decision-making process.

According to the International Data Corporation or IDC, many IoT companies are cerebrating of utilizing blockchain technology with their solutions.

IDC withal expected that around 35% of IoT deployments would enable blockchain accommodations by 2025. This amalgamated prognostication for blockchain and IoT could amplify in the future with the blockchain technology offering a secure and scalable framework to facilitate communication among IoT contrivances. Furthermore, blockchain can additionally enable astute contrivances for executing automated micro-transactions with better speed and cost-efficiency. You can withal optically canvass the possibilities of IoT contrivances utilizing keenly intellective contracts for transferring information or mazuma.

2.7.4.Better Integration of Keenly intellective Contracts and Law

Blockchain technology definitely presents futuristic possibilities with the functionalities of keenly intellective contracts. The rudimentary conception of an astute contract is the automatic execution of certain tasks upon fulfillment of certain conditions. However, it is possible to optically canvass a future where other conditions in astute contracts could withal be subject to automatic regulation.

One of the prominent examples of blockchain future applications in licit applications is the pilot blockchain project by Insurers AIG for the engenderment of intricate indemnification policies. However, it is arduous to find an even ground for disputes between participants of keenly intellective contracts. So, it is plausible to visually examine a future where the rule of law applies to keenly intellective contracts for resolving disputes between the parties.

2.7.5. Blockchain Interconnectivity May Pergrinate to the Next Level

It is definitely too anon to verbally express that we have reached the maximum level of interconnectivity. Concurrently, interoperability is withal essential for ascertaining seamless operations across multiple platforms. Around 83% of organizations believe that assurance of standards and governance for interconnectivity and interoperability among permissioned and permissionless blockchain networks is consequential for joining an industry-wide blockchain network.

Furthermore, virtually one-fifth of the organizations believed governance and standards as essential factors for interconnectivity and interoperability. With incipient technological developments in this field, it is plausible to expect more members requesting guidance on integration among different protocols. Consequently, it is plausible to postulate a possible future in which blockchain platforms do not restrict any enterprise. This can be a crucial factor in driving industry-wide blockchain adoption without any onboarding difficulties.

2.7.6.Financial Sector Would Lead in Blockchain Application

The banking and finance industries do not require radical upheaval of subsisting processes for adopting blockchain technology. Financial institutions are yarely accepting the utilization of blockchain in finance for conventional banking operations. According to a recent study, distributed ledger technologies along with blockchain can avail in abbreviating the costs for financial accommodation providers by virtually $15 billion to $20 billion annually by 2022. In additament, Gartner had prognosticated that the banking industry would leverage blockchain for deriving business value over $1 billion by 2022. So, it is facile to verbally express that blockchain is the future of the banking and finance industry with its exceptional prospects.

CHAPTER THREE

# Physical security measures in banks

## 3.1. Introduction

The financial accommodation sector comprises over 1,200 financial institutions and is a critical component of Singapore's economy, contributing to about 25 to 30 per cent of the country's gross domestic product magnification over the past years. Securing the environment of the financial accommodations sector is a continual and challenging effort. We require to balance between the bulwark desiderata of the sector whilst maintaining the conducive and open business environment that has sanctioned the sector to thrive. Adopting a jeopardy-predicated approach to developing a physical security programme will enable each financial institution (FI) to manage its security risks and aegis needs in accordance with its circumstances and jeopardize appetite whilst maintaining an environment that is conducive for its businesses.

Singapore remains a prime target for malefactors and terrorists to launch attacks on sundry critical infrastructures, with FIs amongst the top targets. Malefactors and terrorists target Singapore for its paramount role in the ecumenical financial industry. FIs in Singapore are typically located in office buildings, retail spaces such as shopping malls and town centres that are typically proximate to conveyance hubs and diligent public spaces. Such locations are typically targeted due to the high human density and are perceived as soft targets by terrorists as compared to a well secured regime facility.

The calibers of aegis recommended in this guideline and in the Ministry of Home Affairs (MHA) Guidelines to Enhanced Building Security in Singapore (GEBSS) establish a substratum reference for the deployment of supplemental protective measures as threat levels increase. However, they do not surmise nor recommend that maximum bulwark is always required as a standard but suggest design considerations and ways of preparing the FIs in enhancing their security posture to meet the threat level when needed. The ABS Guidelines additionally aim to achieve the same objectives as verbally expressed in the Infrastructure Auspice Act (IPA) in accordance with the Infrastructure Aegis Bill relinquished by the MHA in 2017. These objectives cover the aversion of a prosperous attack, minimising casualties and efficacious replication and instauration. FIs are exhorted to review the associated risks (such as loss of life, major business disruption) and apply the indispensable controls as felicitous.

The approach in developing an efficacious physical security programme is predicated on the following four components:

• Threat and Susceptibility Risk Assessment: The process of conducting a Physical Security Risk Assessment and managing of physical security risks through risk identification, susceptibility assessment, impact analysis and imperil treatment.

• Auspice: Protective measures taken to mitigate the identified physical security peril. These quantifications cover Infrastructures, Systems, People and Procedures.

• Detection: The systems and process of monitoring, surveillance, identification and reporting of a security incident or threat information.

• Replication: Actions taken to contain and mitigate the impact as a result of a security incident and to resolve the incident. your bank.

**3.2. Security Measurements**

Albeit many financial malefactions occur online these days, banks are still prime targets for malefactors looking to accumulate information for further cybercrime or commit a bank larceny on site. Consequently physical security measures for banks and credit coalescences are still needed as they remain the number one targets for larceny. Below we outline how banks can further secure their physical space.

3.2.1.Security Specialists on the Ground

Any bank's first line of bulwark is the security specialist at the door meticulously monitoring each person entering and leaving the bank. This simple surveillance technique can eschew and most importantly deter a malefaction from being committed.

3.2.2.Strategically Placed Security

Having adscititious security specialists within the bank avails integrate another layer of security to consistently visually examine suspicious customers and anything that may seem out of the mundane. While less customers are going into physical banks nowadays, the minimized number of personnel make banks an alluring target to those looking to commit a malefaction. In these cases, security specialists should be strategically placed around the bank to view all angles and areas of the lobby to bulwark staff and customers.

3.2.3.Bank Employee Training

Teller security training is another vital factor. Each bank employee should ken what to probe for and how to respond to any type of assailment or threat. Passwords or keys to the vault and other secure areas should only be in the hands of upper management.

3.2.4.Secure Equipment

Bank terminals should never be left authenticated on as someone could facilely walk over and view the data on-screen. Keys to mazuma drawers should always be kept on the teller or secured in a locked cabinet.

3.2.5.Video Surveillance

A vital security feature that must be in place are cameras around the lobby, the ATM machine, and vault areas. A security specialist should be monitoring these cameras throughout the workday. Adscititiously, all the footage should be backed up in the event an incident does occur, ascendant entities will have visual proof and evidence to work from.

3.2.6.Gregarious Engineering Cognizance

Convivial engineering is one way bank purloiners gain access to secure areas, pretending to be someone of ascendancy or a confounded customer. Consequently, all employees must be trained on how to spot these scams, deal with gregarious engineering tactics and respond felicitously.

3.2.7.Access Control and Biometrics

A critical aspect of bank security is access control and biometrics. Banks should implement systems requiring dactylograms or facial apperception afore sanctioning access to secure areas.

Even in the tech age, banks cannot be too punctilious when culling security to forfend their customers and premises. DMAC offers top-notch full-training security personnel. Our eligible specialist are flexible, critical ruminators who remain calm in the face of a crisis. Call today to ascertain more about our accommodations and the high caliber of security we can offer your bank.

**3.3.Threat And Susceptibility Risk Assessment**

Physical Security Risk Assessment (RA) involves the identification of potential threats and assessment of its impact to the organisation with the objective of identifying and implementing felicitous mitigating physical security measures. There are sundry instances when a RA or Threat and Susceptibility Risk Assessment (TVRA) should be conducted as needed by regulatory or internal requisites. The MAS Technology Risk Management (TRM) Guidelines states that the TVRA aims to identify the physical security threats and operational impuissances to determine the caliber and type of bulwark required. RAs may differ in intricacy due to the variants of infrastructure, criticality and scope. The assessment of threats and susceptibilities will vary depending on factors such as geographical location, multi-tenancy considerations and type of tenants, asset and operational value to the organisation, impact from natural disasters, and the prevailing political and economic climate.

The FI should base its RA on sundry possible scenarios of threats under the MHA Peacetime Threat list which includes larceny, explosives, unauthorised ingress, external attacks amongst others. RAs should be conducted in key facilities or critical assets such as Data Centres, Headquarter building/office, flagship branches and critical operational areas.

The RA can be a quantitative or qualitative assessment. The stages of conducting a RA include:

1. identifying and prioritising their assets or operations predicated on the value and criticality;
2. identifying the threat scenarios that are applicable to its operations and assets taking guidance from the MHA Peacetime Threat list;
3. evaluating the susceptibility of the asset or operation due to the identified threats;
4. conducting an impact analysis; and
5. determining the opportune physical security measures to contravene these jeopardies.

FIs should consider conducting a RA of the (re)development of a building or premise; major modification, renovation or alteration arising from an incident or periodically, at least once every five years. A RA may additionally be required as and when requested in accordance with the sundry regulatory requisites such as the MAS TRM Guideline or IPA.

Depending on the desiderata and resources of the FIs, RAs may be conducted either by internal or external security professionals. For RAs involving any critical infrastructures (CI) and High Profile Development (HPDs) that may require the conduct of structural and blast analysis, FIs should consider engaging an eligible Security Consultant / competent person. Guidance on the criteria for determining competent persons or qualified Security Consultants can be referred to MHA. The scope to these RAs may involve technical assessments such as blast effect analysis, structural resiliency studies and developing a security auspice plan as per MHA requisites in the IPA.

Subsequent RAs may be performed by assigned security professionals within the FI's organisation. The RA should be a customary security programme in the FI's security policy to ascertain that security measures and plans are reviewed and updated to maintain pertinence and efficacy (GEBSS).

3.3.1.Susceptibility Assessment

A susceptibility assessment refers to the process of identifying and evaluating gaps or impotencies in the FI's security controls that, if exploited, may result in damage, loss and/or liability for the FI.

During a susceptibility assessment, the subsisting security controls for the FI's asset are being evaluated for potential security gaps, impotencies or non-conformance. Susceptibilities can include deficiencies in security countermeasures, security technology systems, security auspice systems and loss obviation programmes for both the building and the FI's tenanted space. They contribute to the astringency of damage when an incident occurs.

Incipient susceptibilities can arise from:

1. Incipient or escalated threat situation.

2. Deterioration/discontinuation of subsisting capabilities and security systems.

3. Incipient or updated processes/regulations for example incipient regulations or guidelines from

the ascendant entities or incipient organisational goals.

4. Availability of incipient or more cost-efficacious technologies to potential threat actors that were

anteriorly unavailable.

5. Major modification, renovation or alteration to the building or adjoining environment.

3.3.2.Impact Analysis

An impact assessment covers the analysis of the resulting effect or loss to an organization due to the occurrence of a physical security incident. This resulting effect may be in terms of operational and business disruption, loss of assets and information, cost etc. The impact assessment takes into consideration that different assets, processes or businesses and the assessed level of damage or loss may have different value to the organisation. Impact assessments thus provide an organisation with the faculty to appreciate that not all threats pose the same level of peril, and more importantly, it provides a comparative estimate of the relative consequentiality of the threats posed.

In a criticality assessment, criticality is evaluated by studying the impact of consequences associated with the loss or degradation of an organisation's asset in the event of a prosperous attack, breach or exploitation. The extent of peril impact depends on the likelihood of sundry threats and susceptibilities pairing or linkages capable of causing harm to the organization should an adverse event occur. Some prevalent examples by which consequences may be expressed or quantified include financial value/loss; fatalities/injuries; operational downtime; reputational damage; and regulatory impact.

In evaluating the criticality, the following points can be taken into consideration:

1. The value of the asset, activity or function to the FI's operations (tangible or intangible) such as loss of mazuma or disruption of network to branches or ATMs. Assets shall include but not inhibited to people, information and property. The asset value is the degree of the debilitating impact that would be caused by the ravagement or incapacity of the asset.

2. The time frame or duration that the asset, activity or function may be unavailable afore its effects become consequential.

3. Impact on brand, image, reputation arising from negative press or diminished standing in the community.

A criticality assessment may be acclimated to determine resource allocation towards bulwarking assets that are deemed to be more critical in cognation to the threats and susceptibilities faced.

Evaluating Risk

FIs should perform an analysis of the potential impact and consequences of these perils on the overall business and operations. There are numerous methodologies and approaches to integrating the assessments on threat, susceptibility and impact to determine security jeopardy. An example of qualifying the jeopardies assessed is illustrated in the GEBSS

Chart 1: Risk Assessment

(Risk = Threat [T] x Susceptibility of critical asset [V] x Consequences of a prosperous attack [C]).

There is no single definitive approach to imperil assessments as culling a felicitous method depends on the FI's risk management strategy, risk appetite and resources among other factors. Regardless of the methods being used to derive the peril evaluations, FIs should be guided by the following principles for an efficacious RA process:

1. The scope of the assessment should be pellucidly defined.

2. The insights obtained from the assessments should be comprehensible to all parties

involved in the jeopardy management process.

3. The results of the assessment should be actionable such that it distributes consequential

3.3.3.value for its stakeholders.

As a general principle, the RA should be performed on a periodic substratum (at least once every five years) to ascertain that the organisation remains au courant to its security peril, including its threat landscape and the efficacy of associated security measures.

3.3.4.Risk Treatment

Risk treatment decisions are driven by tolerance and acceptable risk levels that are unique to each organisation. Care should be taken to ascertain that addressing one risk does not engender another. FIs should develop and implement risk mitigation and control strategies that are consistent with the value of the assets and their jeopardy appetite level.

Risk mitigation entails a methodical approach for evaluating, prioritising and implementing congruous risk-abbreviation controls. An amalgamation of technical, procedural, operational and functional controls would provide a rigorous mode of truncating jeopardies. Physical access control systems of office ingressions, visitor management procedures at the building's ingress, deployment of sentinels at branches are examples of such controls.

As it may not be practical to address all kenned risks simultaneously or in the same timeframe, FIs should give priority to threat and susceptibility pairings with high risk ranking/rating that could cause paramount harm or impact to the FI's operations. The FI should assess its risk appetite for damages and losses if a given risk-cognate event materialises. The costs of peril controls should be balanced against the benefits that can be achieved.

The FI should maintain a jeopardy register which facilitates the monitoring and reporting of jeopardies. Risks of the highest astringency should be accorded top priority and monitored proximately with conventional reporting on the jeopardy mitigation actions. The FI should update the jeopardy register periodically, and institute a monitoring and review process for the perpetual assessment and treatment of the jeopardies.

3.3.5.BULWARK

The physical security counter-measures will vary for each FI depending on its locality, types of assets and operations. For instance, the quantifications for offices, retail branches and critical facilities such as data centres would differ.

When designing a security concept for the auspice of the FI's premises, it is paramount to consider the cognate spaces and find the right balance between engendering a secure environment and the requisites of the tenanted space. For example, as a shopping mall is open to the public, identifying suspicious characters may be challenging given the diversity of the public as compared to an office building.

With the ascending threat of terrorism ecumenically, immensely colossal and crowded shopping malls are captivating soft targets due to the potential for mass casualties. The associated risks of such an environment should be taken into consideration by the FIs when designing the security bulwark measures of an asset. As an example, a branch placed in higher risk locations should consider incrementing surveillance and detection capabilities or enhancing emergency replication plans in anticipation of such incidents.

Typically, FIs operate in variants of buildings and premises. For example,

Representative Offices or Support Offices are conventionally located in commercial office buildings, Retail Banking Branches in retail spaces, and Essential Accommodations in Critical Buildings or Data Centres. FIs in tenanted spaces should be engaged with the building owner or management to understand the building's Security and Safety Design to orchestrate their own security requisites. These requisites are published in the GEBSS and Appendix – Building Management Engagement Guideline of this document.

3.3.5.1.Key Concepts - Layered Approach to Physical Security Defence

Bulwark refers to measures taken to harden or safeguard an asset from loss or damage. As no single protective measure can minimize or eliminate security risk efficaciously on its own, a auspice in-depth approach comprising of the deployment of layered and complementary controls is commonly utilized in the design and implementation of auspice measures.

Building designs that employ layers of security auspice to eliminate or limit the possibility of an assailment avail abbreviate the desideratum to employ hardening measures across the entire structure and/or in concrete vulnerably susceptible areas.

The layering of protective measures is typically predicated on the following concepts:

• Deter – visible measures that dissuade threat activity;

• Detect – measures that provides the identification or annunciation of threat activity;

• Delay/Gainsay – measures that decelerate or impede the progress of threat activity;

• Replication – measures that react to and interrupt threat activity.

More information is available in the Contingency Orchestrating and Protective Security Advisories for Workplaces document by the Singapore Police Force.

Factors to consider when orchestrating physical security controls include:

1. Infrastructure and the architecture of the facility, which include perimeter boundaries e.g. fences, boundary walls; building perimeter e.g. ingresses for people and conveyances; internal spaces and rooms e.g. public areas, secured offices and restricted rooms.

2. Security systems and electronic contrivances such as alarm sensors, access control systems, turnstiles, video surveillance systems.

3. People, security personnel and employee monitoring and managing access controls.

4. Security procedures and security operations including security incident replication guidelines.

Each auspice measure may be cumulations of functions relating to deterrence, detection, delay/denial and replication. For example, a CCTV surveillance is primarily deployed as a detective control but may withal accommodate as a deterrent function depending on where and how the cameras are being deployed. Similarly, lightings can accommodate to deter malignant activity and may additionally avail the detection of such activities.

A key principle in designing and implementing an in-depth approach to aegis is to layer complementary controls such that it increments the attacker's effort for a prosperous attack or delay its advance so that breaches can be responded to in a timely manner. The general directions presented in the GEBSS are orchestrated according to the following security layers:

1. Deterrence - measures employed are aimed at leading the assailant to cerebrate that his attack plan is liable to fail consummately or will not achieve the results desired. Examples includes the deployment of an auxiliary police officer in retail banking branches, security sentinels in commercial buildings, access control and visitor management procedures.

2. Pro-active security:

a. Pro-active mind-set - to perpetually seek out the potential assailant (Detect), and for security personnel or staff to shift expeditiously from routine to emergency mode (Respond). Training and familiarisation with security procedures reinforces such mind-sets.

b. Pro-active deployment - external detection for possible approaching threats (Detect & Deter). Examples include security sentinel patrol and video surveillance with analytics capabilities.

3. Perimeter security - One of the principles of security is the faculty to detect a suspected assailant as far away from the building as possible or at a point where the assailant would cause the least magnitude of damage. Perimeter security is a critical external ring-fencing function and when not efficaciously utilised, it may cause earnest susceptibilities to a building's security deployment. In many cases, it is the responsibility of the building management to secure the external perimeter. FIs should be mindful of the quantifications that the building has implemented as a component of their overall assessment. Examples include boundary controls to a secured compound, building and shopping mall's main perimeter ingresses, and ingresses for stand-alone branches.

4. Access control - Access control covers sanction and rules by which conveyances, personnel and goods may enter a facility. Access control is a very consequential security feature as most attacks that take place within the facility will cause much more damage and casualties than an assailment which occurs outside. Examples of access control include electronic access control systems for offices and branches, bollards, and turnstiles at critical infrastructure such as the Data Centre.

5. Security command and control room - The security command control room is the nerve centre of security operations and should receive and provide vital information to and from the security personnel on shift, and first responders both in routine and emergency situations. The control

room is typically managed by the building management or building security team but sometimes forms part of the FI's operation. FIs should be mindful of these procedures as a component of their overall assessment and coordination with the Security Command and Control Room during a security incident or any other emergency.

6. Emergency procedures – Security incidents such as terror attacks can be lethal as they develop at an expeditious rate and conventionally occur with no admonition, leading to possible catastrophic results. Time is critical, and the security replication must be immediate, automatic and pre-orchestrated. This is achieved through the emergency and voidance plans. FIs should ascertain that enhanced security procedures that address the replications to these scenarios are available, and that are coordinated with the germane procedures for the building. This provides the assurance that the I can manage the incremented security risks including escalated threat levels beyond business as customary conditions.

The following sections cover the aegis measures on structures, systems, people and procedures in reference to the GEBSS. As the nature of their business and operations among the FIs vary, this section fixates on bulwark measures that are broad-predicated.

**3.4.Infrastructure**

A resilient building infrastructure is essential to minimize the susceptibility of the organization against security threats. Characteristics such as location, environment, natural physical barriers and general infrastructural auspice (e.g. stand-off distance) avail to provide security to staff and businesses.

Most terrorist attacks appear to be perpetrated by planting an IED inside the building or by a suicide bomber infiltrating into it. Employing external security layers is one of the principles of security to detect a suspected assailer as far away from the building as possible or at a point where the assailant would cause the least magnitude of damage.

Another major threat relating to the building perimeter is the facile approach of a potential Conveyance Borne Improvised Explosive Contrivance (VBIED) to the external walls and ingress and ramming through them to enter the main building. The main principle in mitigating such a threat, postulating that consummate aversion is not always possible, is by installing physical barriers at vulnerably susceptible locations to avert the conveyance from approaching a critical proximity and installing blast mitigation elements on glass facades.

These threats should be taken into consideration by FIs as a component of the pre-lease assessment for incipient sites or incorporated into incipient constructions where possible. For subsisting buildings, susceptibilities should be assessed and addressed for the cognate risks to be mitigated.

3.4.1.Stand-off Distance

Stand-off distance is the distance between an asset and a threat, and can be achieved by having an efficacious perimeter line which engenders space between the point of an explosion and the building itself. It is the single most paramount factor when considering the mitigation of the effects of an explosive attack such as VBIED against a building. There is no ideal stand-off distance as it is tenacious by the type of threat considered, methods of construction and the preferred level of bulwark. More details can be found in the GEBSS.

Given the scarcity of land in Singapore and the locality of commercial buildings where bank branches and offices are sited; the application of adopting an immensely colossal buffer zone for stand-off distance might not be practical for most developments. To mitigate this peril, passive enhancement measures such as pellucid/conveyance-free zones, planter boxes, bollards and/or low screen walls can be deployed.

Where indispensable, for critical buildings such as Data Centres, FIs may consider engaging qualified security consultants to review the adequacy of the security measures to mitigate the jeopardies.

3.4.2.Building Perimeter

Buildings should have a well-defined physical perimeter line disuniting secure and nonsecured areas as it is the last defence averting any threats from approaching within perilous proximity of the building. This line can be achieved in many ways depending on the bulwark level required, and the layout of the building.

Where the FI operates in a tenanted space, considerations of perimeter aegis of the office building or shopping mall should not be given only to its immediate tenanted boundary of the office space or branch, but adscititiously for the overall building where the premise is sited such as the ingresses of the shopping mall or office building. For high risk facilities, organisations may consider the utilization of perimeter aegis by utilising fencing or wall barriers. Key considerations such as construct, deployment and height are consequential when evaluating the utilization of security fences or wall barriers.

Besides delaying unauthorised ingression, perimeter bulwark measures should accommodate to dissuade would-be assailants by making it arduous for intruders to surmount without a high chance of failure or detection. Lighting, CCTV surveillance and/ or intrusion detection systems may be deployed to provide supplemental deterrence and/ or increase the arduousness of breaching the perimeter auspice measure.

The extent of perimeter controls should be resolute by the FI's security unit predicated on the susceptibilities identified from the TVRA conducted; and through close coordination with the building management to enhance the FI's own perimeter control measures.

3.4.3.Ingression Points

physical building perimeter establishes a controlled access area around a building or asset. The number of external ingression points including vehicular access should be minimised and congruously controlled. Depending on the assessed threats, denial/delay measures such as gantries or security gates may be deployed to bulwark against unauthorised or coerced ingression.

The GEBSS provides the technical standards and guidelines to these perimeter line design and aegis measures. In integration, the utilization of lighting, CCTV surveillance and intrusion detection systems may be deployed as complementary security measures at ingression points. Exterior doors and windows should be of sturdy and fine-tuned construction, with secure locking contrivances. External glass facades, doors or windows vulnerably susceptible to damage may require adscititious bulwark such as the utilization of tempered glass or shatter-resistant film.

The orchestration to avert unauthorised ingression or to delay intrusion can be developed predicated on the following considerations:

• Where are the ingression points in their building, office, branch and critical facility?

• What are the susceptibilities of these ingress points? For instance, are there multiple ingression points with varying degrees of arduousness in monitoring and control? What are the vigor of construction and materials utilized for ingress point controls?.

• How can these susceptibilities be addressed or mitigated? Can turnstiles or gates be installed?

• Who can the FI work with to enhance the security auspice plans for ingression points? Can the building management and security, or Singapore

Police Force's Safety and Security Watch Group (SSWG) provide assistance?

3.4.4.Walls and Partitions

Walls and partitions accommodate as physical barriers that segregate public areas from non-public or restricted areas and play a major part in the overall bulwark capabilities of the building. It is a consequential line of auspice against explosions, minute arms attack, coerced ingress and other malefaction and terror cognate threats. Ideally, an envelope wall of reinforced concrete should be constructed with segregation between public and restricted areas reinforced with floor to ceiling slab partitioning. This quantification can increment the resistance to coerced ingression into the restricted areas via access under raised floor boards or above the ceiling boards. In additament, security controls such as seismic detectors may be deployed to enhance the detection of intrusions.

There are sundry construction methods verbalized in the GEBSS for building structures, which can be taken into consideration during the design phase for incipient buildings. Depending on the recommendations of the RA and other requisites, a blast shielding wall may be obligatory on certain components of the building as well as a reinforcement of glass facades and structures.

3.4.5. Internal Access Points

All internal access points should be designed with the felicitous level of security, depending on the sensitivity of the area. As with exterior ingression points, internal access points should be complemented with other measures such as lighting, CCTV surveillance and door access control hardware (including secure locking mechanisms). Off operational hours security controls should be considered when designing the access controls.

Adscititiously, access points to restricted or critical areas should be designed with complementary controls such as 2-Factor Authentication (2FA) as well as intrusion detection systems and/ or audible alarm systems. Depending on the jeopardy assessment, specially designed bulwarked ingresses such as gates, interlocking systems or portals may be required to delay coerced-ingression. The GEBSS has recommendations for the different calibers of security, namely, Rudimentary, Medium and High.

3.4.6.Special Facilities

3.4.6.1 Vault/Vigorous Room

A vault or vigorous room is a room that is designed for the safekeeping of valuables including cash and negotiables. Depending on the valuables kept and containment limits set by the FI, the vault should be constructed to meet the minimum internationally acceptable standards. Each vault should have a lockable day gate to avert unauthorised ingression during operating hours and a vault door equipped with dual access control contrivances such as coalescence lock and key. CCTV surveillance and/ or intrusion detection systems may be deployed to provide adscititious deterrence and/ or increase the arduousness of breaching the vault perimeter. The intrusion detection system should be monitored to facilitate prompt replication to any security alerts or breaches.

3.4.6.2 Critical Equipment Room

Critical equipment is defined as assets that are essential for fortifying the facility's operations and includes machines that support electrical power supply, dihydrogen monoxide supply, air supply, communications systems and networks as well as fire auspice systems. As these equipment or utilities may be critical to facilitating emergency replication in an assailment, their ravagement could cause harm that is disproportionate to the building's damage from the direct attack. For example, if a fire breaks out from an explosion, the consequences of the fire aegis system failure could be higher than the direct impact of the explosion.

Critical equipment should be located away from areas assessed to be of higher peril, concealed and bulwarked. The rooms housing the critical equipment should be built with adequate auspice such as CCTV surveillance, door access control hardware and systems and intrusion detection systems among others. In integration, access should be restricted to sanctioned personnel only.

If these critical equipment rooms are a component of the building's infrastructure that are managed and maintained by the building management, the FI should include them in its risk assessment to withal assess them as a component of the overall infrastructure fortifying the FI's security programme.

3.4.6.3 Mailroom

Mailrooms handle the building's mail streams including receiving and storing mails, parcels and distribution items until they are accumulated or re-distributed. If such rooms are not congruously designed and located, it can present a threat to the building and its occupants when mail items are utilized as an expedient of chemical, biological, radiological and explosive (CBRE) attacks. For this matter, mailrooms should ideally be located near the ingression to the building or in a separate facility within the building away from critical areas and key structural elements such as the building's structural columns or transfer beams. For safety reasons, mailrooms should withal have dedicated air handling units or ventilation system, taking into consideration the design and cost elements.

The area where incoming mail and parcels are being screened should be designed to mitigate blast effects. As mailrooms are high risk areas, the room should be built with adequate bulwark such as CCTV surveillance and door access control systems. In additament, access to the mailroom should be restricted to sanctioned personnel only.

In some instances, FIs may not have an in-house mailroom and may receive mail from third party accommodation providers or couriers. They should recognise that they are may be exposed to the same level of threat from incoming mails, and the pertinent mailroom security training should be a component of the pro-active security to identify and detect such threats for escalation and replication.

**3.5. Systems**

The opportune deployment of security systems may enhance the FI's protective capabilities on its assets. Security systems are conventionally utilized for the following purposes:

- Detecting and providing an element of deterrence against illicit activities and intrusions.
- Admonish security personnel of belligerent activity and/or breaches of security.
- Monitor activity in sensitive or vulnerably susceptible locations.
- Recording activities for future review or investigations.

In deploying security systems, it is paramount to not rely on a single technical measure. Instead, security systems should be deployed in a manner such that the controls achieve a complementary and layered approach to asset auspice.

It is withal consequential to note that security systems have relatively moderate life spans. It is consequently advisable to design the system to enable periodic changes and updates to ascertain the operational readiness of the system. In additament, FIs should additionally undertake the felicitous hardening measures when designing systems to be bulwarked against cyber-attacks.

More information on the design, cull and designation of security systems is available in the GEBSS.

3.5. 1 CCTV Surveillance System

A CCTV surveillance system is an integral part of security monitoring as it provides information for investigative work when the desideratum arises. Depending on where and how CCTV surveillance is deployed, it withal accommodates to deter threat actors if they perceive that their actions are being monitored and recorded.

The opportune placement of CCTV surveillance contrivances should be predicated on the perils identified. Typically, they are deployed at access, remote or vulnerably susceptible perimeter points, areas of critical business operations and areas containing high value or critical assets such as:

- Building perimeter.
- Fence line or boundary lines.
- Conveyance access points.
- Building/Branch ingressions.
- Building/Branch lobby.
- Vaults.
- Access control points and screening points.
- ATM/ATM lobby.
- Sensitive/restricted office ingress.
- Critical equipment rooms.
- Technology rooms.
- Data halls.
- Security control room.

In integration, it is consequential to ascertain that blind spots are being adequately covered by CCTV surveillance and that the amassment, utilize and disclosure of CCTV recordings must be in accordance with the Personal Data Bulwark Act (PDPA).

CCTV recording equipment should be kept in a secured facility which is accessible only by sanctioned personnel. This is to obviate tampering to the equipment settings or video recordings. If the CCTV surveillance system is a component of the building's infrastructure managed and maintained by the building management, the FI should withal assess them as a component of the overall infrastructure fortifying the security programme in its risk assessment.

For more technical information as well as general concepts and design considerations, FIs can refer to the GEBSS and Video Surveillance System (VSS) Standards for Buildings published by the Singapore Police Force.

3.5.2 Door Access Control System

Efficacious access control ascertains that kineticism is regulated by determining access into categorical areas for sanctioned persons. Maintaining an efficacious door access control system is a fundamental principle of good access control management. When designing an efficacious electronic access control system, the GEBSS recommends the following considerations:

• The number of ingresses should be prioritised and minimised.

• The areas with restricted access such as external doors that should be closed to the public.

• The access control system should not compromise the fire auspice and safety systems. Electronically controlled doors should be integrated with the fire aegis system, for example, to relinquish the secure door for emergency egress in accordance to local fire code. Fail-secure design electronic locks are recommended for such doors.

Access control should be established at all germane and congruous ingress/ exit points within the organisation such as building ingress, office ingresses, and perimeter doors. More vigorous access control measures should be deployed at sensitive or critical areas of the office/ building such as cash processing area, safe rooms, sensitive document storage rooms and data halls.

This may include the utilization of two factor authentication (2FA) access controls systems such as card and PIN, or card and biometric, enabling anti-pass back function, and/or utilizing interlocking door access controls (or man-traps).

3.5.3. Intrusion Detection and Alarm System

Intrusion detection and alarm systems are aimed at detecting and annunciating unauthorised intrusion and/ or coerced ingress into a secure area. It is paramount that an efficacious deployment Physical Security Guideline for Financial Institutions Page 16 of 43 of intrusion detection and alarm systems must be complemented with monitoring and replication methods. The intrusion detection and alarm system include a variety of perimeter, internal and external alarm detection/ triggering contrivances (such as kineticism detectors, seismic detectors, door contacts, duress buttons). The system is programmed to monitor sundry parameters, which may include aperture of doors, crossing of perimeter line or kineticism in a defined space. Upon activation, the system will engender a local alarm and/ or transmit the alarm signal to a monitoring centre for follow-up replication actions. For more technical information, FIs can refer to the GEBSS. For high risk areas, redundancy for the alarm communication channel should be incorporated in the alarm system. The system should be additionally equipped with independent back-up power source and a control panel located in a secured area. If the intrusion detection system is a component of the building's infrastructure managed and maintained by the building management, the bank should assess them as a component of the overall infrastructure fortifying the security programme in its risk assessment.

3.5.4. Preventive Maintenance and Servicing

Preventive checks and accommodation maintenance of security equipment and systems should be conducted customarily to ascertain that the performance of these systems and equipment are maintained at an optimum level. There should be plans to ascertain that designated persons utilize the felicitous systems with congruous controls such as utilizer profiles and utilizer rights. These orchestrations should include procedures on the abstraction and eradication of any data such as CCTV recordings (e.g. the abstraction or eradication of faulty recorder hard disks by vendors) and guidance on personal data bulwark. For security systems managed and maintained by the building management, the FI should assess them to ascertain that they are consummate, as a component of the overall infrastructure fortifying the security programme in its risk assessment.

**3.6. People**

As security is everyone's responsibility, people play a crucial role in bulwarking an organisation and its assets. People shape the environment and culture to engender a pro-active mind-set, one of the security layers advocated by the GEBSS to promote vigilance against threats and replication to security incidents.

3.6.1. Employees

Efficacious security depends on the comportment and mind-set of employees. To develop vigilance and a heightened security mind-set amongst employees, FIs should have security cognizance and training programmes. These programmes should be designed according to the roles undertaken by the employees. Core components of security training include information on the type of applicable threats and imperil issues, how to identify suspicious persons and activity and what is expected of the employees to detect, obviate and respond to potential security issues. Such training can be conducted face-to-face, via online platforms or through exercises, while cognizance programmes can be distributed through newsletters, brochures, posters, bulletins or information packs.

3.6.2. Security Officers

A pro-active approach can enhance security while minimizing the opportunities for potential attacks. Security officers should adopt a pro-active mind-set to perpetually seek out potential assailers and respond to security incidents promptly. Customary germane training should be conducted to provide security officers with multiple skills to enable them to detect terrorists and pre-attack reconnaissance. All security officers must be licensed or exempted by the Police Licensing and Regulatory Department and should be screened afore they are culled for employment. Prior to employment, security officers must be felicitously certified through the Security Workforce Skills Qualifications programmes. Upon employment, all security officers have to be perpetually trained in security and safety cognate procedures, including but not circumscribed to, emergency replication and voidance procedures, bomb call/hoax procedures, suspected mail bomb/ article replications, rudimentary initial fact-finding procedures, rudimentary fire-fighting and rudimental first avail. Security personnel are required to conventionally participate in drills and exercises to familiarise themselves with the applicable security procedures and replications for the building.

3.6.3. Mailroom Personnel

As mailrooms are considered high risk areas, all mailroom personnel should be trained on the procedures to identify, respond and escalate any mail cognate threats and other suspicious items. If these personnel are outsourced, FIs should ascertain that the accommodation provider adequately trains their employees on the indispensable procedures and the building's emergency plan for a coordinated replication to handle threats.

**3.7. Procedures**

Procedures provide guidance and operating protocols to manage physical security situations. Some prevalent procedures relating to the management of personnel and electronic security measures are:

3.7.1. Security Standard

Operating Procedures FIs should ascertain that a current and updated set of Security Standard Operating Procedures (SOPs) is available. The SOPs should incorporate the building's SOPs relating to the day-today security operations management to the management of escalated security incidents. This will ascertain that the FI's SOPs complements the building owner's when responding to security incidents. The SOPs should include considerations for the sundry threat scenarios assessed in the RA and the different Security Threat Level to orchestrate for the germane replications and resources required.

3.7.2. Door Access Review

A conventional review of door access privilege should be conducted on a conventional substratum to ascertain that the physical access rights of employees are valid. For sensitive or critical areas, the FI should review the door access log records to check for potential access contravention or suspicious activities. Visitor Management Visitor management procedures involve the identification, management and tracking of visitors. Visitors should be directed to a registration point at the building or office for identification and screening utilizing felicitous photo identification. During the screening process, visitor details should be recorded either into the visitor management system or record book for tracking purposes prior to issuance of visitor passes. Where compulsory, visitors should be accompanied by sanctioned personnel from the organisation. If the visitor management system is managed and maintained by the building management, the FI should assess them as a component of the overall security programme risk assessment.

3.7.3. Sentinel Tour Management

Procedures on sentinel tour management ascertain a systematic approach to the patrolling of premises and the provision of adequate security coverage within all strategic and vulnerably susceptible areas such as ingression points, critical equipment rooms, staircases, and accommodation areas. This would include the scheduling of sentinel tour timings, routes and checkpoints. As a good practice, sentinel tour frequency and routes should be varied to eschew predictability. If the sentinel management system is managed and maintained by the building management, the FI should assess them as a component of the overall security programme risk assessment. DETECTION One of the key elements of a security programme is detection. Detection refers to the monitoring and surveillance of an organisation's immediate physical premises, circumventing environment and assets to identify security incidents prior to or when an incident occurs. An example of detection is the utilization of perimeter CCTV surveillance to detect intruders endeavoring to scale a perimeter fence or breach a door. Through early detection, FIs will be able to carry out timely replications to manage the security incident and mitigate its impact. Detection measures should be in place for both tranquility-time and heightened security conditions. System detection can involve both on-site and off-site monitoring to achieve a more robust detection outcome.

**3.8. System Detection**

System detection include the deployment of video surveillance, intrusion detection and access control systems to detect physical threats, illicit activities or intrusions. It admonishes designated personnel of potential bellicose activity and/or breaches of security and avails monitoring of activities in sensitive or vulnerably susceptible locations. The recordings from the system can facilitate post investigations or be utilised as data to be analysed as a component of security astuteness accumulating. Adequate lighting in the exterior and interior of the premises is additionally consequential to avail in the identification process upon detection of potential threats. Please refer to Section 2 for more information on the sundry security systems.

**3.9. Monitoring**

System detection should be supplemented with active monitoring so that congruous actions can be taken to respond to detected threats. Monitoring is typically performed by an off-site third party Central Monitoring Station (CMS) or an on-site Security Control Room (SCR)/Security Command Centre (SCC). The CMS and SCC are the nerve centres where the field contrivances of the detection systems are connected to triggering alerts which provide vital information for the replication personnel in both routine and emergency situations. A typical security control room should contain all of the main operating stations of the security systems installed throughout the facility. To efficaciously monitor the alerts, the security control room personnel needs to have a clear circumstantial cognizance with the competency to prioritise and filter pertinent information received from CCTV surveillance and the alarm system so as to efficaciously differentiate genuine incidents from erroneous alarms. The SCR should be equipped with an escalation plan to guide the security personnel on actions to be taken when a threat is detected such as who to notify and escalate. Working surfaces should be designed to enable SCR personnel to have a good view of the CCTV monitors. For more information, please refer to SPF's VSS Standards for Buildings and the guidelines on Image Presentation and Authentic-time Surveillance. FIs should consider having different escalation plans to suit the variants of premises (i.e., data centre, retail branch, office buildings etc), to detect security incidents. It is consequential to have detailed escalation and replication plans to ascertain that congruous actions will be taken to mitigate the threats upon detection.

Please refer to Section 4 for more information on Replication.

**3.10. Detection**

Strategies (On-site In-house/Building Management and Off-site Monitoring) Different detection strategies for on-site in-house/building management monitoring and offsite monitoring could be deployed depending on the criticality of the premises and whether the premises are owned by the FI. For instance, if a FI is the sole tenant or in a plenarily owned building or a standalone Data Centre, an on-site in-house monitoring security control room could be established to monitor, detect and escalate a security incident. An FI in a multitenant premises will likely be dependent on the on-site building management security control room or to establish off-site monitoring either by an in-house security team located in another location or by a third party security vendor. 3.3.1 Detection through People and Assessment Detection by trained security officers and employees is a utilizable betokens to identify suspicious persons, activities and items. The general roles played by security officers and employees are mentioned in Section 2. Fundamental security cognizance programmes should be implemented to train employees to look out for suspicious persons loitering in the banking hall or office premises and to escalate to the on-obligation security personnel or security department. Security personnel and employees should be trained and briefed on the escalation procedures covering who to notify and escalate if there is any security issue in the premises. In integration, please refer to GEBSS for more details on tell-tale designations of suspicious objects and the Dos and Don'ts of handling such objects. Detection Approaches during Placidity-time and Heightened/ Enhanced Security Conditions The FIs should develop different detection approaches for tranquility time and heightened/ enhanced security conditions. Detection approaches during tranquility-time are covered in the preceding narrative on security systems such as video surveillance, intrusion alarms and access controls utilized in conjunction with active monitoring by the security control room or third party monitoring centre. These quantifications are supplemented by the people in the FI such as on-site security personnel and/or employees to lookout for any suspicious persons or items. Detection approaches during heightened or enhanced security conditions will be in integration to the placidity time security measures depending on the FI's internal risk assessment. The FIs would require to take into consideration if the premises are owned, partially owned or leased. FIs which own or have full control of the premises, could implement incremented or enhanced security measures to detect suspicious persons/conveyances during heightened security or as exhorted by the ascendant entities. These may include circumscribing ingress/exit points (lockdown procedures), deploying of supplemental security personnel and conducting bags and/ or vehicular checks or screening. Broadcast to employees could withal be undertaken to raise their cognizance and to mitigate any potential threats. FIs, in a multi-tenant building, co-location data centre or with inhibited control of the premises should consider working with the building management to complement their internal security plans with the building management security plans to mitigate any potential threats in a heightened or enhanced security situation.

**3.11. Security Astuteness**

Astuteness detection consists of tracking, monitoring and reporting of threat information or perspicacity on issues that could engender risks to the organisation. The provision of timely, precise and objective astuteness accommodates to prepare the FI against identified threats and avails to guide security decisions and actions in managing the organisation's risk management approach. The astuteness cycle which comprises of four phases – orchestrating and direction; information accumulating; analysis; and dissemination, provides a broad methodology for threat astuteness.

3.11.1. Orchestrating and Direction

The first phase of the astuteness cycle is the orchestrating and direction stage, which sets the organisation's astuteness priorities. This phase entails accumulating and understanding the requisites regarding the type, depth and priority of the information to be amassed and the information accumulation methods. By plenarily understanding the requisites, a monitoring plan could then be developed to monitor the threats. An information accumulation plan may be habituated to designate and track the progress of the mentioned requisites, including potential information gaps.

3.11.2. Information Amassing

The second phase of the perspicacity cycle relates to information accumulating or accumulation. Depending on the perspicacity requisites, the required information may be amassed from a range of sources including internal and external as well as open and closed sourcesInformation can additionally be amassed through online platforms such as advanced web searches (including websites, blog), Boolean queries (utilizing keywords and coalesced with operator words), open source alerts (such as RSS aliments or Google alerts), analytic implements (keywords, mapping) and geo-fencing. Other information sources include media reports, commercial vendor reports, public databases, the law enforcement ascendant entities), peregrine embassies, peer organisations and regulators. FIs are enheartened to participate in national forums and initiatives such as the Safety and Security Watch Group (SSWG) Scheme that provides sundry platforms for information amassing and sharing.. In additament, organisations may additionally establish networks with industry peers and obtain customary communication on industry-concrete security issues via security or industry cognate sodalities. Seminars, conferences or workshops withal provide opportunity for accumulating insights on security-cognate issues and to establish networks with subject matter experts. Where congruous and pertinent, and subject to the FI's policies and guidelines on information sharing, financial institutions are emboldened to apportion non-sensitive information and/or perspicacity with pertinent industry peers on a timely substratum so that opportune actions can be taken.

3.11.3. Information Analysis

After the information is amassed, the security department should, predicated on the organisation requisites, the information is then analysed, identify information of value, placed in the germane context and used to assess the potential threats and jeopardizes to the organisation by the security department.

3.11.4. Dissemination of Perspicacity

The dissemination phase includes a communication plan which will identify the germane stakeholders and senior management to receive the information, how and when the astuteness is disseminated and method of reporting such as email, inscribed briefs and/or with threat maps. As a general principle, astuteness should be disseminated in a timely manner to the germane stakeholders and senior management to facilitate the initiation of felicitous actions and replications by the organisation. REPLICATION Replication refers to protective actions taken to mitigate a security incident or an emergency, as well as actions taken to react to a physical security threat. All replication approaches can be framed into three main phases: 1. Preparation; 2. Incident Replication; and 3. Post Incident Recuperation.

### 3.12. Preparation

Preparation is paramount in managing a security incident or emergency efficaciously. The preparation phase involves developing plans and procedures to deal with the security threats and jeopardize issues that are being identified by the FI. In developing a replication plan, FIs should consider assigning roles and responsibilities to personnel as required during an incident, identifying the points and modes of replication activation, developing concrete procedural guidance to dealing with the identified threats as well as accounting for assets and people. The preparation phase additionally involves working with the germane stakeholders such as the building management to align operating protocols and procedures. Emergency orchestrating for buildings and office premises must be tailored to different situations. There are numerous physical security measures that can be taken for security and emergency preparedness. These include deploying visible security cameras, kineticism sensors, security personnel, locking contrivances and developing a comprehensive security operations plan. Staff should be trained to increment the caliber of security vigilance. Towards this end, training programmes should be implemented on how to identify and report suspicious persons, items or activities . In additament, staff should withal be trained in handling threatening telephone calls or bomb threats. Customary security-cognate exercises and drills should be conducted so that employees and role holders are perpetually updated and made vigilant of the sundry emergency replication procedures. Building management staff should consider conducting a study of susceptibility issues in the structural resiliency of the property and essential utilities. Adequate physical security measures should be implemented to bulwark the building and mitigating procedures to ascertain that their critical business components are amply bulwarked against terror attacks targeting the infrastructure of the premise.

3.13. Personnel Security

Personnel management is a key component in a physical security incident. Efficacious management of an incident requires all emergency replication personnel to be pellucid of their roles and responsibilities so that they can carry out their sundry functions swiftly and efficaciously. Staff must be accounted for efficiently when an voidance is activated. The pertinent department responsible should have a system or policy to expeditiously commence accounting for employees when required so that everyone in the organisation is accounted for. Staff needs to be perpetually updated and their sentiments and morale managed when a security cognate incident occurs. The organisation and the Human Resources department should provide the compulsory counselling to affected employees if needed.

3.14. Protocols

Protocols such as SOPs, emergency plans and guidelines avail the organisation to be organised and better prepared to face any security incident. These customarily involve developing and implementing policies and SOPs cognate to physical security incidents. Engendering staff cognizance and training on physical security programme are paramount to ascertain that all protocols and germane information are disseminated to the pertinent staff. To further augment these efforts, conventional security simulation exercises should be conducted to invigorate these protocols by identifying and addressing gaps, if any, in these orchestrations. 4.4 Incident Replication Swift action is required to mitigate any damage arising from incidents. Roles, responsibilities and actions to be taken should be limpidly defined. This should include coordination and liaison with the germane external ascendant entities if an incident is escalated. The incident respondent or Emergency Replication Team should first identify the cause of the incident or breach and ascertain that incident is contained. This prompt action ascertains that measures are taken to mitigate further impact and eschew any inadvertent compromise of the integrity of any follow up investigation. Replication protocols for individuals in the following situations should be developed and simulated:

- Active Assailant
- Bomb Threat
- Mail Distributed Threats
- Chemical, Biological and Radiological Threats
- Person-Borne Improvised Explosive Contrivance (PBIED)
- Conveyance-Borne Improvised Explosive Contrivance (VBIED)
- Hostage Situation

3.14.1. Active Assailant

The guiding principles for individuals to respond to an active assailer threat are “Run, Obnubilate and Tell”: 1. Run when it is safe to do so:

- Consider the safest route.
- Move expeditiously and mutely.
- Stay out of view of the assailers.
- Insist others leave with you.
- Leave your paraphernalia behind.

2. Obnubilate if you can’t run:

- Find cover from the assailer and stay out of optical discernment.
- Lock yourself in but do not get trapped.

• If you are unable to lock the doors or ingressions, place objects such as tables and cupboards abaft the doors or ingressions to obviate access by assailers.

• Move away from the doors.

• Be very mute and switch your mobile contrivances to mute mode.

3. Tell the Police when it is safe to do so

• Give your location and where you last visually perceived the assailers.

• Provide details about the assailants.

3.14.2. Bomb Threat

Call When a bomb threat is received:

1. Do not panic. Stay tranquil.

2. Alert someone to call the Police. Keep the caller occupied by verbalizing as long as possible while the Police traces the call.

3. The officer receiving such calls should threat them earnestly and immediately endeavor to determine:

• the precise location of the bomb and precisely how it looks homogeneous to;

• the detonation time and what will it set off;

• the amount and type of explosive used; and

• the reason for such an act.

4. lt is additionally consequential to take note of the following:

• the caller's voice and vocal characteristics (e.g. pitch, male/female, adult/child);

• the language used and accent (e.g. local or peregrine);

• manner of verbalizing (e.g. expeditious, deliberate, emotional, irate);

• background noises (e.g. traffic, music, public promulgations, shouting);

• the person or ascendancy whom this message should be conveyed to;

• do not antagonise or taunt the caller in any way; and

• be polite and remain placid.

5. Do not spread rumours.

6. Depending on the situation, voidance or invacuation replication may be annunciated. Follow the procedures as applicable.

3.14.3. Mail Distributed Threads

Threat Bombs/explosives can be distributed through the postal accommodation or courier. Most bombs are designed to detonate when the outer wrapping is cut open or torn. If you receive a mail item such as a letter/parcel suspected of containing explosives, do not endeavor to open it but instead take the following actions:

1. Call the Police.

2. If you are not sure of the inception of the mail item but have reasons to suspect that it is a bomb, treat it like a bomb and alert the Police.

3. Place the suspected mail item in a corner of the room away from windows.

4. Evacuate the room and building if obligatory, leaving all the doors and windows open. This is to sanction the blast if any, to vent and mitigate the deleterious effects of the shattering glass.

5. Authoritatively mandate all personnel and evacuees not to physically contact anything that looks suspicious while securing the premises. 6. If an explosion occurs and voidance is affected, give opportune injuctive authorizations to redirect the evacuees to safer/alternative routes of escape.

3.14.4. Chemical, Biological, Radiological (CBR)

Threat If an item is suspected of containing CBR material, the individual should take the following actions:

1. Do not handle the letter or package suspected of contamination. Do not shake or empty the contents of the article.

2. If any of the contents (e.g. powder) is spilled from the article, do not endeavor to emaculate it up. Expeditiously, cover the area where the powder was spilled with a congruous item (e.g. apparel, paper, trash-can, etc) to avert it from spreading. Do not abstract this cover.

3. Switch off nearby fans or ventilation units in the proximity of the affected area.

4. Leave the room and close the door or block-off access into the area to obviate others from coming proximate to the affected area. 5. Wash your hands with soap and dihydrogen monoxide to avert further spreading of the powder.

6. Abstract contaminated habiliments as anon as possible and put them in a plastic bag or a congruous container that can be sealed and have them available for the Police/Singapore Civil Defence Force.

7. Shower with soap and dihydrogen monoxide as anon as possible. Do not utilize bleach or other disinfectants on your skin.

8. List the denominations and contact numbers of all the persons who were in the room or area, especially those who had direct contact with the powder. Give this list to the Police for follow-up investigations and the issuing of felicitous medical exhortation/follow-up for individuals who had contact with the powder.

3.14.5. Person-Borne Improvised Explosive Contrivance (PBIED)

PBIEDs are explosives that are concealed on-person, either under or within apparel, shoes, or other types of apparel and can result in mass casualties if detonated in crowded areas. When posed with a PBIED, the individual should:

1. Stay tranquil.

2. Crawl under a sturdy table or a solid object if things are falling around you, and remain there as long as it is safe to do so.

3. Stay away from glass or fixtures, like windows, mirrors, cabinets, and electrical equipment.

4. Follow the orders of the Police or safety personnel. If an voidance is injuctively authorized, leave the building as anon as you can.

5. Do not go near fire hazards.

6. Once out of the premises, keep as far away from the building as possible.

7. Do not utilize elevators.

8. The best place to be in an event of an explosion is to stay flat on the ground.

3.14.6. Conveyance-Borne Improvised Explosive Contrivance (VBIED)

A car bomb, lorry bomb, or truck bomb, withal kenned as a conveyance-borne improvised explosive contrivance (VBIED), is an improvised explosive contrivance placed inside a car or other conveyance and detonated. The individual should take the following actions in a VBIED situation:

1. Stay placid.

2. Obnubilate abaft a solid object or wall and remain there for at least few minutes as there may be a secondary blast.

3. Stay away from glass or fixtures, like windows, glass panel or doors or electrical equipment.

4. Do not utilize your mobile phone.

5. Follow the orders of police or security personnel.

6. Keep far away from the blast as possible.

7. If you are injured stay flat on the ground and wait for medical avail.

3.14.7. Hostage Situation

Hostage situations can transpire at any time, anywhere. The element of surprise and capricious nature of these assailments make them one of the hardest situations to prepare for. If you are taken hostage:

1. Remain serene, be polite and cooperative.

2. Do not endeavor to be a negotiator.

3. Verbalize only when you are verbalized with and in a mundane manner.

4. Comply with all orders and ordinant dictations.

5. Do not make sudden bodily forms of kineticism, pass comments or cast truculent visually examines the captor(s).

6. Scrutinize the captor(s) and memorise physical traits, voice pattern, apparel and other details that will avail the ascendant entities.

7. Stay low to the ground or behind cover from windows or doors if possible

3.14.8. Post Incident Review

In the post incident review, FIs are to analyse the root cause(s) and identify gaps in incident replications and susceptibilities in the physical security plan. Parties involved in the incident replication may want to conduct a self-assessment of their performance and replication gaps. Inputs from stakeholders should be sought and used to assess the efficacy of protocols and identify the scope as well as desideratum for future cognizance training. FIs may conduct a physical security risk assessment as a component of the post incident review to identify amendments in physical security systems and infrastructure. Plans should be developed and implemented to ascertain that corrective actions are taken to address the identified gaps and enhancements to the security measures. These edifications learnt should be incorporated into your policies and procedures.

CHAPTER FOUR

# Cybersecurity standards for automotive

## 4.1. Introduction

As with many industries, the automotive sector is becoming increasingly dependent on computer technologies to provide the performance and differentiating features expected of its products. The magnification of connectivity and contrivances which can be updated in-situ makes in the security of such technologies (cybersecurity) crucial.

The possibilities of risk presented by cyber attack will depend on the potential outcomes, and the factors that determine the likelihood of an assailment. In the automotive industry, the outcomes can be astringent – elongating to a chance of injury or death if a safety-cognate function is compromised or to a major reputational loss if an astronomically immense class of conveyances is threatened or needs to be recalled.

The commercial context is, however, arduous: security is concerned about the avoidance of an outcome (a prosperous attack) that might never occur. Such factors are generally arduous to make into positive differentiators (with the exception of some premium brands, perhaps).

"Security is a hard-to-evaluate feature against a possible future threat, and consumers have long rewarded companies that provide facile-to-compare features and an expeditious time-to-market at its expense."

The fundamental challenge is not incipient: cybersecurity threats have subsisted as long as computers have been utilized in sensitive applications, and wide-spread attacks on networks have been public cognizance for proximately 30 years. Industries face these issues in different timescales and environments according to their caliber of dependence on computer technology, the rigor of the impact of a cybersecurity attack, and the size and perceived value of the target they present. We have optically discerned, for example, more stringent security measures brought into place in the aerospace and energy industries: these offer some edifications for the automotive sector, but edifications that need to take into account the sector's unique economic and regulatory environment.

This paper addresses challenges and best practices around cybersecurity in the automotive industry, concentrating on the incrementing utilization of computer-cognate technology in the conveyance and its environment. The 'enterprise' cybersecurity challenges that automotive businesses share with any commercial enterprise in other sectors are addressable, but are best discussed elsewhere. Our target audience is thus the managers and architects responsible for the product (in research and development functions) and those responsible for the product's perpetuated presence in the market (e.g. in after sales support and maintenance management).

**4.2. Automotive Cyber Security Challenges**

Addressing automotive cybersecurity requires facing a number of challenges which are categorical to the industry and which accommodate to make the cybersecurity issue more arduous than in some other industries.

Incrementing cars volume ecumenical and higher intricacy of car's electronic systems is perpetually growing.

Indeed, in-conveyance software and system/network architecture are more and more involute and Connectivity/ interfaces are multiplying with the external world.

•The intricacy of car's electronic systems is perpetually growing and driven by the expedition of the market requisites. The market expects the car to be safe, not only by forfending its occupants but additionally by obviating accidents. This is achieved by electronic driver assistance systems (e.g. parking, speed regulation, lane, and blind spot detection, pre-collision). The car is withal expected to be more comfortable (e.g. automatic cooling, seat adjustment with recollection, automatic tailgate opening, and performance control) and to provide a consummate infotainment system (e.g. navigation, audio, voice assistant, Bluetooth). Car manufacturers are providing more integrated value accommodations requiring network connections (e.g. emergency calls, remote diagnostic, remote support, internet browsers, and concierge).

Modern cars have to provide to their users a continuum in their live. People want to be aeonianly connected to get sundry information and additionally to interact with their convivial and professional ecosystems.

These requisites lead to automotive electronic architectures which are growing expeditiously in involution and which are immensely colossal even in comparison to other industries [4]. The average modern high end car software is 100 million lines of code, to be compared with Windows 7 (39.5 million in 2009) or a Boeing 787 (13.8 million). Having so many lines of codes implicatively insinuates that some susceptibilities very likely subsist and represent security issues.

•Amount of connected cars is growing expeditious

In an ecumenical market growing by more than 70 million cars per year, the magnitude of connected car will grow expeditious. This will significantly increase the assailment surface hackers might exploit.

The reasons why they are susceptibilities in software are diverse. It appears that the management of astronomically immense automotive projects is not always cognizant enough of the paramount and specificities of cybersecurity. One of them is linked to the fact that developers of software in the automotive sectors are not acclimated to take into account security since the commencement of the project. They consider they are not enough trained and that there is not enough opportune security enabling technologies in the processes they utilize. Security cognizance, and active management of security policy at high calibers in an organization, is additionally typically a challenge for industries facing incipient cybersecurity threats.

Licit and regulation reinforced to establish a collective pressure to ameliorate auspice

Another lever that accentuates security in automotive is the evolution of the regulations. To take one single example, the European General Data Aegis Regulation (GDPR) will be efficacious in May 2018. Mastering data privacy in conveyance will be a challenge considering the ascending quantity of data stored and managed in a conveyance and between the conveyance and ground bases. The challenge will even be higher for rented cars, fleets and car sharing accommodations. Indeed, privacy cognate data might be stored and shared for technical or commercial purposes. The customer must be formally apprised and must substantiate his consent. This might become involute when accommodations are distributed by third parties and cognate amassed data sold for integrated value accommodations.

Modern society cannot accept anymore that security incidents impacting end users be kept obnubilated. There is an ecumenical trend of the regulators to oblige organizations make security incident publicly kenned. One of the reasons is that making information public will lead to establishing a collective pressure to amend auspice. Without this pressure, who kens if the amelioration would be performed?

Regulation requires that some repair and maintenance information (RMI) has to be facilely and pellucidly accessible to promote competition in the conveyance repair market. This limits some of the quantifications available for managing and controlling security.

**4.3. Safety And Financial Impacts Due To Its Susceptibility**

•Impact of cybersecurity on safety: having connected the car to the external world engendered incipient risks.

Systems that were designed for years as being plenarily disconnected and exchanging information exclusively within the car– when on the move - have been connected to billions of contrivances, computers and objects across the world. Despite the fact that the security of some of these connections may be invigorated by car makers or OEMs, the situation engenders incipient risks. What if the embedded systems driving the brakes, assuring geo positioning or ascertaining lane following would be corrupted? This might lead to a contingency with consequences potentially impacting persons conveyed by the conveyance, but additionally people and goods located in the circumventing environment. Ergo the connection of the car leads to drastically influence safety. What might be optically discerned as a security issue – illegitimately accessing and modifying data in conveyance – is now a safety issue. Security and safety must converge for our best interest.

•Lack of commonly accepted standards for development and accreditation

In order to prosperously address security in a connected world, all stakeholders should apportion a prevalent understanding of how to manage security: what is security, how to implement it, how to control it, what are the processes and organization obligatory to manage it? In diverse industries, information security management and implementation is described in standardized best practices documents. There is not yet such a widely apperceived set of reference documents for the automotive industry. Some best practices and standards subsist but are not covering the full life cycle of security management and are not yet widely apperceived by all industry players. This engenders sundry side effects at industry level, as engineering involution, maintenance and integration issues, intricacy of monitoring and investigating to designate a few. This requisite needs to be a top priority for car manufacturers, suppliers, and stakeholders imperatively.

•Financial and image impacts can be heftily ponderous

Most of the security incidents impacting cars are reported within hours. The relinquished news customarily associates the incident to the car maker that appears on the headlines across the world. This is not to verbalize that the impact on the image is major, most of the car makers having be in this situation are still remuneratively lucrative. But it is to verbally express that no major incident has occurred yet. The public opinion might change when it will occur.

**4.4.Categorical And Growing Threats And Hackers Motivations**

Software is never perfect and it is commonly postulated that there are few susceptibilities in connected cars software (as in most of other industries). Susceptibilities are exploited by assailers to perpetuate malevolent acts. In 2016, two security researchers demonstrated that Jeep's digital system can be facilely hacked remotely over the Internet. The found susceptibilities were exploitable on a plethora of other conveyance brands which utilizes the same regalement system such as Dodge. This hack cost a lot to Fiat Chrysler as the group image tarnished; 1.4 million conveyances being affected and recalled afterwards. The more software, the more susceptibilities and the higher is the jeopardy that information might be glommed, transmuted or expunged out of the control of the car maker. The motivations of assailants have already evolved. Whilst some years ago they were mainly composed of researchers, journalists and freelancers who wanted to demonstrate incipient hazards, they nowadays are very liable to include structured organizations (licit or not) with adept resources and consequential budgets. It is plausible to fear that in the future E-mafias will expect to engender sizably voluminous gains through attacks which present low risks to the assailant.

Gains are potentially high because of the quantity of conveyances and their value cost. Currently, the peril to the manufacturers and operators of conveyances is still held low because of the potential capability to assail remotely utilizing connectivity interfaces with public networks is circumscribed, but withal because of the desideratum to be physically near the car to conduct efficacious attacks (e.g. jamming signals or eavesdropping exchanged keys between ECUs and OTA key apps). Transmutations in conveyance connectivity abstract some of these coincidental bulwarks, however.

### 4.5. Secure Automotive System

As an answer to these cybersecurity challenges, threats, and susceptibilities, an ecumenical security strategy needs to be defined. Cybersecurity is definitely an incipient topic in the automotive industry; auspiciously there are mature technologies, implements, but additionally edifications learned, and processes in other industries and markets that can be acclimated and reused.

There is no desideratum to reinvent the wheel; however some unique product-cognate characteristics need to be taken into account. For instance, one difference with IT networks and personal/commercial computers is the desideratum to forfend conveyances operations as well as data and system components. This is a well-kenned safety-security issue which is categorical to critical infrastructures and environments.

Withal, car lifecycles, which are considerably longer compared to traditional computer products, have indisputable impact on security processes such as firmware and software update strategies. It is pellucid then that the industry has a desideratum to establish a germane list of best practices that should be venerated to ascertain a secure design in the long run. These best practices will avail to reinforce the overall security and keep the final product safer.

### 4.6. Dedicated Cybersecurity Standards For The Automotive Industry

A well-established standard is always an assurance that processes and implementations are compliant with best practices and guidelines. Several efforts have already been undertaken in order to provide such cybersecurity guidelines for the automotive industry, ecumenically but withal country-concrete. The overlapping risk is an authenticity and all these standardization bodies need to coordinate with each other to eschew conflicts and ambiguities. Local initiatives include for instance the EVITA (E-Safety Conveyance Intrusion Bulwarked Applications) project in Europe which aimed to provide in-conveyance reference architecture predicated on HSM.

The Japanese IPA (Information Promotion Agency) conveyance information security guide covered a terminus-to- end lie-cycle of the conveyance including third-party and suppliers demeanor toward security. More recently, international standardization bodies such as ISO (International Organization for Standardization) and SAE (Society of Automotive Engineers) joint their effort to work on the definition of a dedicated cybersecurity standard for the automotive industry. SAE already initiated these works internally within the Conveyance Electrical System Security Committee where the J3061 cybersecurity guidebook and the J3101 requisites for hardware-forfended security documents are engendered. ISO's TC22 and SAE are additionally identifying the potential interactions between system safety and cybersecurity.

Altran fortifies the drive to develop a single and prevalent security process for automotive. Establishing a shared terminology and unique standard that can be macrocosmically utilized by stakeholders, third party suppliers, developers and car manufacturers, it avails in raising the overall vigilance around the topic and inculcates a 'built-in' security culture within the industry. Altran additionally shares the interest for collaborating with other security standardization activities in other industries such as astute convey systems or IOT. Edifications learned from kindred past experiences are always remuneratively lucrative and utilizable.

**4.7. Defense In Depth Principles**

The bulwark in depth principle is one of the cybersecurity core pillars nowadays. It has already been applied in several fields, especially in critical infrastructures such as aeronautics or industrial systems.

Indeed, paramount assets need to be forfended utilizing a multilayered security approach in order to abbreviate the impact of a prosperous intrusion. Similarly, it is certainly a good practice to utilize multiple security countermeasures to mitigate risks in connected cars, in case an intruder is able to get access through several breaches. A security framework for automotive should be then built upon a bulwark in depth strategy including:

•Secure interfaces with the external world (e.g. OTA, driver dedicated applications, OBD, Bluetooth). Indeed, these interfaces can be optically discerned as an explicit invitation to hack a conveyance system as several exploits already subsist on them. They should be major points of interest and a priority for automotive architects when the security policy is being designed,

•In-conveyance secure network architecture providing physical segregation and isolation of safety-

cognate ECUs utilizing secure gateways and communication buses (e.g. CAN, Ethernet, FlexRay),

•Hardware Security Modules (HSM) which provide a vigorous security anchor for software by bulwarking fundamental security functions (e.g. secure boot, key generation, key storage, active recollection aegis) for microcontrollers. HSM avail to distribute hardware security accommodations such as trusted Execution Environment (TEE) or cryptographic computing expedition for better performances,

•Secure the supply chain as several actors are customarily involved in connected car system design. All the stakeholders need to be vigilant of the cybersecurity risks to be mitigated and act accordingly by following guidelines and best practices they are concerned with,

•End-to-end security strategy by bulwarking the chain-of-trust from the car architecture to the servers and the cloud.

4.7.1. Security By Design Applied In Every Step Of The Project Lifecycle

Security by design betokens that security is taken into account in every step of the project lifecycle starting from designations to validation. As an example, secure coding rules sanction developers to rely on vigorous security practices while their code is engendered, evading innate susceptibilities such as buffer overflow.

Haplessly, embedded software developers customarily neglect security engineering best practices and need to be more vigilant of the jeopardies they are facing. An ecumenical top-down security strategy needs to be defined to consummate such an objective, covering management, operations, maintenance, third parties, car manufacturers, and suppliers.

Security by design implicatively insinuates additionally that a 'built-in' security is thought at early stages of the design of the car system, compared to a 'built-on' security where security is integrated block by block to counterfeit incipiently discovered security breaches. A good security-by-design policy should then cover:

• Organizational methods for secure development, by conducting for instance reiterated risk assessments on most critical components in the car system,

• Secure management of cognate projects, providing security requisites and technical solutions,

• Security verification and validation, subsisting security development lifecycle frameworks such as ISO/IE 27034 can be reused and acclimated to achieve security-by-design in automotive systems (e.g. perforation testing, static code analysis).

4.7.2.CStrategies For Countermeasures To Abbreviate Attacks And Bulwark Car System

In order to truncate the assailment surface and forfend most critical assets in a car system against the variety of threats discussed above, several efficacious state-of-the-art security countermeasures can be applied such as:

•Secure in-conveyance communications utilizing mature COTS cryptographic products for primary

functions such as onboard network segregation, intrusion detection, or data filtering,

•ECUs hardening by reverencing best practices such as effacing interfaces and accommodations utilized for development when the car is yare for release, or utilizing a tradeoff amalgamation between hardware and software security to leverage bulwark-in-depth. These practices should be applied to every ECU, even those which are not critical to the conveyance operation,

•Perform customary survey on cybersecurity evolution (both from an intrusion and bulwark perspective) in homogeneous keenly intellective conveyance systems such as Aeronautics where the embedded context is commensurable to in-conveyance networks (e.g. partitioned operation systems, domain segregation, convey operation criticality),

•Rely on technology diversity to contravene security monoculture. The conception is to do not put all eggs in the same basket: diversity, when opportunely applied, is a practical implement to evade attack propagation to critical components,

•Maintain security over time utilizing surveillance techniques such as perpetual susceptibility management or firmware and software updates utilizing out-of-band channels. Additionally, security maintainability is a key enabler for a long-term cryptographic-predicated bulwark. It is unlikely to have a cryptographic key vigorous enough to last as long as the conveyance lifetime; these systems should be then thought with such constraints in mind.

Security, and concretely cybersecurity, is an increasingly clamant issue for the automotive industry, as systems become more technologically involute and the threat environment additionally becomes increasingly capable and sophisticated.

The criticality of this issue will only be intensified by trends such as highly-automated & autonomous driving and V2X communications. A rational approach to security can be predicated on a construal of peril – an amalgamation of the astringency and the likelihood of prosperous attacks.

A range of best practices subsist and can be applied: from management focus down to technical measures can avail control this jeopardy. Prospects of best practices and performance in this area are still evolving, both in terms of industry standards and in terms of market prospects.

Achieving efficacious security requires engagement and monitoring throughout the whole supply chain. The automotive industry has made paramount progress in recent years in establishing mundane prospects for functional safety; security is a cognate topic and an indispensable substratum for safety, so that we may hope to gain both efficacy and efficiency by considering mundane intrigues and edifications learned across these domains.

These conclusions may seem daunting if addressed in isolation and without benefit of prior cognizance – nevertheless we do consider that the business opportunities enabled by adequate security can be achieved by considering practices from across in the industry and edifications learned in other industries as a component of an open professional discussion of needs and approaches.

CHAPTER FIVE

# Security breaches of remote working

## 5.1.Introduction

A data breach - sometimes kenned as a cyber security breach, data leak, or data spill - occurs when sensitive, confidential, or forfended information is accessed by an unauthorized person or persons, physically or digitally.

This data could include:

Personal information such as denominations, addresses, medical histories, etc.

Employee account passwords & credentials

Client or target contact lists

Company strategy documents

Physical papers containing business plans & forecasts.

There are several types of data breaches, including phishing, man-in-the-middle attacks, denial-of-accommodation attacks, password attacks, malware attacks, and even non-malevolent human error.

Human error is one of the most mundane causes of data breaches. It conventionally involves employees sending sensitive information to the erroneous person, which is facilely done when working remotely. Whether it's fortuitously CCing an unrelated party or annexing the erroneous document to an electronic mail, this type of data breach can be profoundly damaging to a business.

However, like every type of data breach, there are ways to mitigate risk and keep your business' data safe. Learning about cyber security best practices is the best place to commence.

Since the pandemic, working from home has become much more widespread ecumenical. Even once the pandemic fades, many presage that remote working will remain prevalent across multiple sectors.

While working from habitation is convenient and has many benefits, it withal exposes both individuals and businesses to a range of cybersecurity jeopardies. That's why it is essential to give solemn consideration to home cybersecurity. By following best practices, you can mitigate most cybersecurity work from home threats quite facilely.

During the COVID-19 pandemic, a paramount increase in the number of employers who offer employees the possibility to work remotely has additionally been facilitated by national approaches to ameliorating the epidemiological situation, which prescribed remote work for all whose work specifics sanction it. At the same time, cyber threats have incremented during the pandemic, which highlights the desideratum to adjust the approaches of employers to cyber-risk management.

The cyber risks and challenges raised by the COVID-19 pandemic and elongated utilization of remote work, as well as risk management approaches or controls introduced. The cybersecurity risks and challenges for companies and organizations associated with transmuting employee habits while working remotely during the COVID-19 pandemic.

When working remotely, not only the bulwark of work information is consequential, but withal the aegis of personal information. The study analyses the cybersecurity risks associated with transmuting employee habits in the transition to remote work during the COVID-19 pandemic.

**5.2. Safety measurement of working from home**

With the ascension in remote working, certain cybersecurity threats – in particular, phishing – have become more prevalent. A key issue is that, in most workplaces, an IT team will take care of cybersecurity within the office. With a distributed workforce working remotely, staff have to pay more attention to cybersecurity threats themselves. Here are the top remote working security tips to ascertain you and your staff are working from home safely.

5.2.1. Utilize antivirus and internet security software at home

One of the most efficacious security tips for working from domicile is to invest in a comprehensive antivirus suite for you and your employees.

According to sources, the estimated ecumenical damage to businesses due to cybercrime is around $1.5 billion per annum. This figure is only liable to increment as hackers look to exploit people's home internet networks and business VPNs to gain access to sensitive files.

These assailments could leave you, your business, and your employees open to ransomware attacks, DDoS attacks, malware, spyware, and other types of breaches.

Antivirus suites take the strenuous exertion off your hands by offering automatic remote work security against a host of threats, including:

Zero-day attacks (viruses capitalizing on security imperfections afore they are patched)

Malware, spyware, and viruses

Trojans and worms

Phishing scams, including those sent via email

Not only can a comprehensive antivirus suite, such as Kaspersky Total Security, fend off up to 100% of online security threats, but it additionally automatically updates itself to stay on top of incipient and emerging threats.

It withal runs discreetly in the background of your other operations, so you won't even notice the strenuous exertion it's doing.

5.2.2. Keep family members away from work contrivances

While you may trust yourself and your tech-savvy employees to forfend themselves online, it's worth recollecting that working from home betokens company computers are more liable to be exposed to puerile children and other members of employees' families.

Ergo, it's paramount to remind staff to keep their contrivances safe and not sanction other household members to access their work laptops, mobiles, and other forms of hardware. It's additionally worth reminding them of the consequentiality of password forfending their contrivances to obviate third parties from accessing sensitive files.

5.2.3. Invest in a sliding webcam cover

Working from home customarily denotes taking part in teleconferences and video calls which require the utilization of your webcam. Infelicitously, savvy hackers can facilely access your webcam without sanction, compromising your privacy. Worse still, if you have sensitive documents around your physical workspace, hackers may be able to view these by hijacking your webcam.

If your webcam is discrete from your contrivance, you should unplug it whenever you are not utilizing it. If your webcam is built-in, you should take extra measures to bulwark yourself – there's no telling when a webcam assailment could occur.

Sliding webcam covers are facile to find online in all shapes, sizes, and colors to suit your desiderata. They are typically facile to install, additionally, as most come with an adhesive layer that fits around your webcam.

While utilizing videoconferencing software, you may withal want to utilize functions such as the "blur background" feature if your platform retains it. This can avert people in your conferences from spying on objects in the background of your abode, which can often include sensitive data about you or your clients.

5.2.4. Utilize a VPN

Remote working often denotes connecting your computer to the company's Virtual Private Network (VPN connection) – but this, in turn, engenders incipient home office safety 'back doors' that hackers could potentially expose.

First and foremost, it's essential to provide employees with work from home security tips and guidance or policies on being a secure remote worker. Companies should probe for ways to make their VPN more secure.

VPN security can be enhanced by utilizing the most robust possible authentication method. Many VPNs utilize a username and password, but you may want to contemplate upgrading to the utilization of perspicacious cards. You can additionally enhance your encryption method for VPN access, for example, by upgrading from a Point-to-Point Tunnelling Protocol to a Layer Two Tunnelling Protocol (L2TP).

Of course, it doesn't matter how vigorous your VPN is: if an employee's password is compromised, it will give hackers a facile way in. So, it's essential to ascertain employees are updating their passwords customarily. You should additionally remind employees only to utilize the VPN when they require it, switching it off if they are on their work contrivances for personal use in the evenings or on weekends.

While working from home, employees will be utilizing their abode networks and internet connections. Ergo, it is a good conception to edify employees how to configure their wireless routers and personal firewalls and keep their abode networks secure.

And, of course, comprehensive security and antivirus software will withal cover your VPN.

5.2.5. Utilize a centralized storage solution

If your company relies on cloud or server storage, you should ascertain all your employees are utilizing this solution. If you feel your employees are not cognizant or acclimated with your storage accommodation, or are perpetuating to store files locally, communicate with them to ascertain they are habituated with the centralized accommodation. That way, if your company is compromised and local files are disoriented, ravaged, or compromised, you are more liable to have a back-up of obligatory documentation. This method withal betokens that consequential documents are safer, as they will be bulwarked by the firewall annexed to your centralized storage solution.

Working from home - Secure your domicile wireless network

5.2.6. Secure your habitation Wi-Fi

One of the simplest ways to ascertain cybersecurity for remote workers is to fortify your habitation Wi-Fi network's security. You can achieve this through some straightforward steps.

Engender a vigorous, unique password, rather than relying on the automatic password your router came with. You can access your router's settings page by inscribing "192.168.1.1" into your browser and transmute the password there. Ascertain to cull a password that would be arduous for anyone to conjecture. You can withal transmute your SSID, the designation of your wireless network, on the same settings page to make it more arduous for third parties to identify and access your abode Wi-Fi network. Do not utilize your denomination, home address, or anything that could be acclimated to identify you.

Ascertain you have enabled network encryption, which can conventionally be done under the security settings on your wireless configuration page. You will have several security methods to cull from, such as WEP, WPA, and WPA2. The most vigorous, if you are utilizing more incipient hardware (more recent than 2006), is WPA2.

You can circumscribe network access to categorical MAC addresses for supplemental security. Every contrivance that connects to your network has a unique MAC address (you can find the address for each contrivance by opening Command Prompt, if you retain it, and entering "ipconfig/all"). If you ken the addresses of verified contrivances, you can integrate these to your wireless router's settings so that only those contrivances can connect to your Wi-Fi network.

Determinately, ascertain you are running the latest version of your firmware by customarily visiting your router setting page. Patches and software updates often address potential security concerns.

5.2.7. Beware of Zoom and video conferencing

Remote working often denotes relying on videoconferencing software – which, in turn, engenders potential WFH security peril.

For example, in the past, Zoom was compelled to address security imperfections after a spate of soi-disant "Zoom bombing" attacks. In these assailments, uninvited persons gain access to another person's video conference and enter it to dismay and harass other users. Albeit the term "Zoom bombing" derives from the Zoom app, kindred incidents have taken place on other platforms.

The risks to your company are that, if your video conferences are being invaded and monitored, sensitive information about your business or your clients may be leaked. Your staff may additionally suffer personal and potentially traumatizing attacks from hackers.

In replication to Zoom bombing attacks, the FBI relinquished exhortation to avail users forfend themselves while utilizing video conferencing software. This includes:

Ascertain meetings are private, either by requiring a password for ingress or controlling guest access from a waiting room.

Consider security requisites when culling vendors. End-to-end encryption offers paramount privacy and security – so check whether any video conferencing software you utilize includes this feature.

Ascertain software is au courant by installing the latest patches and software updates.

5.2.8. Ascertain your passwords are vigorous and secure

One of the simplest yet often overlooked ways to bulwark yourself when working from domicile is to invigorate your passwords and ascertain that you have maximized password bulwark across your contrivances.

The US Federal Trade Commission offers this exhortation,

"Use passwords on all your contrivances and apps. Ascertain the passwords are long, vigorous, and unique: at least 12 characters that are a amalgamation of numbers, symbols, and capital and lower-case letters."

They additionally recommend integrating a password screen every time you access your laptop and other contrivances so that if your contrivance is breached or falls into the erroneous hands, it will be harder for a third-party to access your sensitive files. We recommend utilizing a password manager implement to avail keep all your passwords secure.

5.2.9. Bulwark your online banking

If you are responsible for business accounts, it is essential to ascertain that mazuma is being stored and transferred in the safest ways possible. The last thing you optate is to encounter a security breach in any of your online banking platforms.

First and foremost, it's essential to utilize only accredited software and accommodations to handle mazuma. Utilize only accommodations you ken and are acclimated with. If you are unsure about the credibility of a particular platform, search online for reviews and more information afore utilizing it. Credible institutions should include information for human contacts on their websites, people who customers can verbalize with if they have any concerns.

When accessing a banking website, ascertain you are authenticated on via a Secure Hypertext Transfer Protocol. This denotes the URL should include https:// rather than just http:// at the commencement. You should additionally optically discern a lock on the left of the URL bar of most internet browsers, betokening that website has an authenticated security certificate.

You can increment the security of your business and personal bank accounts by tightening passwords, integrating memorable information, and, if possible, asking your bank for a card reader to ascertain that all online payments require a physical payment card. If you can switch to mobile banking, many platforms now require a verified dactylogram to authenticate, which can enhance security even further.

Hackers, scammers, and phishers may endeavor to target you via email, gregarious media ads, or over the phone. They may request your bank details on the substructure that they optate to avail you make astronomically immense purchases or donations. Do not give your bank details to anyone, or transfer funds to any unsolicited vendors, unless you are absolutely sure that they are who they verbally express they are.

Recollect that scammers may endeavor to mimic your colleagues, clients, or professional organizations, including your bank, to chicane you into giving away sensitive information or transfer mazuma. Be vigilant, and don't be trepidacious to ask anyone for supplemental proof they are who they claim to be.

5.2.10. Be wary of email scams and your electronic mail security

Emails are essential for communication between colleagues. However, emails are withal one of the most facile betokens of communication to exploit and compromise.

The UK's National Cybersecurity Centre (NCSC) has made numerous recommendations for availing forfend staff while working from home, including in the utilization of emails.

As well as calling attention to phishing scams which are becoming more prevalent, they exhort the following measures for bulwarking email accounts:

Ascertain emails can only be accessed securely via your company's VPN, which engenders an encrypted network connection that authenticates the utilizer and/or contrivance and encrypts data in transit between the utilizer and your accommodations. If you already utilize a VPN, ascertain it is plenarily patched.

Staff are more liable to have their contrivances glommed (or lose them) when they are away from the office or home. Ascertain their contrivances encrypt data while at rest, which will forfend email data on the contrivance if it's lost or purloined. Most modern contrivances have encryption built-in, but encryption may still need to be turned on and configured.

Beware of phishing attacks which appear to be taking an ever-growing number of forms.

**5.3. Working from Home Security Tips for Staff**

In summary, to ascertain working from home safely, remote workers can utilize these tips as a checklist:

Are you utilizing a comprehensive antivirus and internet security software at home?

Have you secured your contrivances – by bulwarking them from family members and ascertaining that encryption is turned on and configured? Have you enabled "Find my device" and remote wipe on all your contrivances?

Have you invested in a web cam cover? If your webcam is external, do you unplug it when not in utilization?

Are you utilizing a VPN?

Have you secured your habitation Wi-Fi?

Have you ascertained that your passwords are vigorous and secure?

Are you alert to the hazards of phishing scams, eschewing clicking on links or opening affixments in any electronically mails you are unsure of?

Are you utilizing a fortified operating system, and do you keep your operating system au courant?

Do you keep all software au courant?

Have you enabled two-factor authentication where congruous, or considered the utilization of an authenticator app such as Google Authenticator or Authy?

During video calls, do you take care not to over share your screen and are you mindful of what might be in the background?

Working from Home Security Tips for Employers

Employers considering remote work security best practices can utilize these tips as a checklist:

Do you have a documented work from home security policy? A good example from the Information Commissioner's Office can be found here.

Do you have a BYOD (Bring Your Own Contrivance) policy?

Do you provide cyber security cognizance training to employees?

In particular, do you train staff to be vigilant to phishing attacks and how to eschew falling victim to them?

Are you ascertaining that staff utilize a VPN, and is this establishment opportunely and kept au courant with security patches?

Is the platform you utilize for staff video teleconferencing secure with end-to-end encryption?

Do you utilize a centralized storage solution – i.e. safe data storage in the cloud – and enhearten staff to backup data conventionally?

Are company contrivances secured by company-approved antivirus software?

Do you embolden employees to have vigorous and safe passwords, and have you considered the utilization of a Password Manager?

Do you embolden the utilization of two-factor authentication to validate credentials?

Do you utilize encryption software to forfend company data by barring access to any unauthorized users?

Do you exhort staff to utilize corporate email solutions and not to rely on their own email or messaging accounts for the storage or transmission of personal data?

As working from home has incremented ecumenical, cybersecurity for remote workers has become a sultry topic. By following cybersecurity remote work best practices, individuals and organizations can eschew risks and ascertain safety.

### 5.4. Impact of the Hybrid Workforce on Cybersecurity

Remote working has become commonplace for organizations of all sizes and shapes since the commencement of the COVID-19 pandemic. This change has engendered consequential work from home cybersecurity jeopardies. As such, organizations and employees must understand essential security tips to prosperously habituate to this way of working and minimize the security risks associated with remote working.

As companies rushed to deploy cybersecurity for remote workers in March 2020, cyber malefactors additionally took action. Hackers capitalized on the incrementation in security gaps engendered when many organizations failed to follow remote work security best practices.

For example, INTERPOL, in its assessment of COVID-19's impact on cyber malefaction, found a consequential increase in the number of critical infrastructure, regimes, and astronomically immense organizations targeted by hackers. Between January and April 2020, it detected 48,000 malignant Uniform Resource Locators (URLs), 907,000 spam messages, and 737 malware incidents cognate to COVID.

These figures reinforce the desideratum for organizations to perpetually train their staff on how to maintain security when employees work remotely.

**5.5. Types of Security Risks with Work From Home**

When employees use unsecured networks and contrivances to perform their jobs, such as free Wi-Fi networks, they leave gaps in cybersecurity for malefactors to exploit. Consequential security issues with working remotely include:

Ransomware

Ransomware is a type of malware in which cyber malefactors lock or block users' access to their own data or contrivances. Hackers typically seize control of a machine then threaten to efface, eradicate, or publish data unless their ransom demand is paid.

The primary objective of ransomware is to extort or scam victims. They are often spread through phishing emails containing maleficent affixments that infect a contrivance and then encrypt files or even entire contrivances. Other ransomware attacks use gregarious engineering or drive-by downloading, which sends victims to spoofed websites that install maleficent material onto their machines.

Impuissant passwords

One of the most immensely colossal threats to companies' remote workforces is the perpetual utilization of impotent, insecure, or recycled passwords and authenticate credentials. Failure to utilize secure passwords negates cybersecurity software and implements like firewalls and virtual private networks (VPNs).

Hackers can now use software to avail them crack account passwords and access sensitive corporate information. For example, they can compile prodigious lists of mundane passwords to access accounts or indite code that utilizes multiple password variants to conjecture authenticate coalescences prosperously. Another mundane approach is to utilize passwords they ken someone has utilized for one account, such as a personal email or convivial networking site, to endeavor and access their corporate account logins.

File sharing

Remote-predicated workers are liable to utilize file-sharing accommodations to send documents and files to their colleagues. These files, when stored on corporate networks, are liable to be bulwarked through encryption. However, when shared remotely, the same level of security may not apply.

Sharing sensitive information through file-sharing implements can leave data vulnerably susceptible to being intercepted or glommed by hackers — especially while data is in transit. The loss of sensitive corporate data can result in security events like data larceny, identity fraud, and ransomware attacks.

Unsecure Wi-Fi

Corporate Wi-Fi networks are typically secure because they are forfended by secure firewalls that monitor and block malevolent traffic. However, remote-predicated employees may connect to corporate networks and systems from unsecured Wi-Fi networks.

For example, most people routinely update their smartphone firmware or antivirus software but infrequently do so on their habitation routers. This can leave their domicile network vulnerably susceptible to a data breach that, in turn, risks the security of corporate data.

Personal contrivances

One of the most paramount security risks of remote working is utilizing personal contrivances to connect to corporate networks and systems. These contrivances often do not have the same level of cybersecurity as a corporate computer or laptop. Personal smartphones often do not utilize encryption to bulwark personal data, and home printers can leave security gaps that can be exploited by hackers.

Employee Cognizance and Training on Security Threats with Work From Home

Organizations' employees are the first line of bulwark in obviating security threats with work from home environments. Employers must provide training to increment employees' cognizance of the perils they face and the potential designations of a cyberattack.

Ascertaining a clear understanding of how to maintain security when employees work remotely entails inculcating users on the desideratum to perpetually keep optical discerners open for potential phishing scams. This denotes eschewing links and affixments in emails, especially messages that emanate from unrecognized or unorthodox senders.

Supplemental security tips include:

Utilizing comprehensive antivirus software to secure contrivances utilized for work and that connect to a habitation Wi-Fi network

1. Securing contrivances with encryption
2. Covering laptop webcams and abstracting external webcams
3. Utilizing a ZTNA solution to access applications safely and securely
4. Utilizing secure, vigorous, and unique passwords
5. Evading the utilization of software that has not been approved or licensed by the organization
6. Keeping contrivances and their software and operating systems updated
7. Utilizing authentication applications and technologies
8. Remaining cognizant of screen activity on video callsies and organizations

**5.6. Best Practices and Technologies for Securing**

Home-predicated workers can stay secure and forfend their personal and corporate data by following established remote work security best practices.

Best security practices for working from home employees

The following cybersecurity best practices will avail employees keep their contrivances and networks safe from cyber malefactors:

Secure home networking

Home networking is inherently less secure than networks that employees connect to in a corporate office. Wi-Fi routers come with a default password that is often relatively facile for hackers to crack. Remote workers should set a unique password, which they can facilely amend through the router's settings page by inscribing the router's address, such as "192.168.1.1," in their web browser. This additionally enables users to transmute the denomination of the network—or accommodation set identifier (SSID)—to make it more arduous for a hacker to identify and access the network.

Home networking should additionally be fortified with network encryption, which can be transmuted in the security settings of the router's wireless configuration page. The most robust encryption setting on most routers is Wi-Fi Forfended Access 2 (WPA2). Further steps to fortify Wi-

Fi include constraining access to categorical media access control (MAC) addresses. The router should withal always run the latest firmware version available.

Use antivirus

Antivirus software avails ascertain remote worker security. Cyber malefactors target home networks utilizing advanced attack vectors like distributed denial-of-accommodation (DDoS), malware, ransomware, and spyware. Antivirus software avails fight these threats by automatically detecting, identifying, and obviating viruses, phishing scams, and zero-day attacks from perforating the network.

A comprehensive antivirus solution is equipped with automatic updates so it is vigilant of and obviates the latest emerging security threats. In turn, it sanctions organizations to automatically secure remote work contrivances and workers.

Use internet security software

In integration to antivirus, remote workers should deploy comprehensive internet security software—such as products like cloud backup, identity larceny auspice, password managers, secure web browsers, and VPNs—to bulwark their contrivances.

Use vigorous and secure passwords

Every account must have a unique password that has not been utilized for any other accommodation, is at least 12 characters long, and uses an amalgamation of letters, numbers, and special symbols. Users should additionally consider a password manager, which sanctions them to utilize more robust, unique passwords for their many accounts without having to recollect them all.

Practice email security

The prodigious magnitude of cyberattacks come through email, so it is crucial to have email security in place to forfend employees' communication with colleagues, customers, and partners when working from home. This includes ascertaining email accounts are only accessed via a VPN, which encrypts users' connections, contrivances, and data in transit. Users withal need to remain vigilant by understanding the characteristics of phishing emails and eschewing links and annexations in messages.

Top technologies that ameliorate organization's cybersecurity in the COVID Era

The COVID pandemic expedited the desideratum for organizations to deploy solutions and implements that avail employees work from anywhere as securely as they did in the office. Work-from-anywhere cybersecurity tips for employers include:

Identity management and authentication

Relying on passwords alone is no longer enough to keep cyber malefactors at bay. Instead, users need to integrate an extra layer of security to their online accounts by utilizing identity management implements like two-factor authentication (2FA) or multi-factor authentication (MFA). These implements use sundry authentication methods, such as one-time passwords (OTPs), which verify a user's identity and ascertain a hacker cannot access an online account even if they manage to purloin the password.

Endpoint security solution

Endpoint security solutions bulwark every endpoint connected to an organization's IT infrastructure. Actions they perform include:

- Providing organizations with enhanced overtness of all the contrivances across their networks
- Enabling advanced aegis and dynamic access control
- Detecting and blocking security threats in genuine time
- Automating and orchestrating timely replications
- Fortifying security incident investigation and management

Zero-trust network access (ZTNA)

As the hybrid workforce perpetuates to work from anywhere, the perpetual verification of all users and contrivances as they access corporate applications and data is required. Zero Trust Network Access (ZTNA) forfends networks and applications, network administrators by implementing a zero-trust access.

Data loss aversion

Remote work increases the jeopardy of data being disoriented or glommed during cyberattacks. Data loss aversion (DLP) implements enable organizations to detect and obviate data breaches, contingent data sharing, and maleficent larceny. They block sensitive data from being extracted by unauthorized entities, which is crucial to internal security and complying with increasingly stringent data privacy regulations.

Utilizer behavioral analytics (UBA)

With employees working from disparate locations, it is more consequential than ever for organizations to understand what they are doing. Utilizer deportment analytics (UBA) sanctions businesses to keep tabs on the applications users launch, their network activity, the files they access, and the electronic mails they have sent. UBA additionally analyzes how frequently users carry out concrete tasks and searches for utilization patterns that can denote suspicious or malignant demeanor.

Security information and event management (SIEM)

SIEM avails organizations mitigate the ever-incrementing volume of threats they face circadianly. The technology sanctions businesses to keep pace with the growing deluge of malignant activity, as well as triage and investigate alerts relating to suspicious comportment. SIEM solutions analyze security events to enable expeditious threat detection and replication.

Encryption

Encryption secures data on corporate networks and communications between remote-predicated employees. It transforms data into a ciphertext that can only be read or deciphered by the sender and their intended recipient. This ascertains that a cyber-malefactor cannot read the pristine data, even if they manage to intercept it. Encryption additionally avails organizations ascertain data authentication and integrity as it can prove that data has not been altered from its pristine state.

The cybersecurity can withal be concluded that the methods used to widen the field of work may prosperously lead to consequential ameliorations and that Durex can avail engender more preponderant prospects in the future. If the company is exhorted, it will be able to put them into practice actions to enhance its position in the ecumenical market. By taking all these precautions, Durex should be able to consolidate its leading position in the international market. In this case, some suggestions may be offered as solutions. The utilization of robust security software has the potential to be lucrative since it will secure the safety or bulwark of the firm. Another consequential proposal that must be offered is the modernization of the company's hardware and software, which will avail in minimizing the occurrence of a variety of interruptions inside the business.

www.ingramcontent.com/pod-product-compliance
Ingram Content Group UK Ltd.
Pitfield, Milton Keynes, MK11 3LW, UK
UKHW021922190726
13853UKWH00002B/794

9 798887 836065